My Perfect Companion

Because love is blind

William A. Horsburgh

MY PERFECT COMPANION © 2026 WILLIAM A. HORSBURGH

William A Horsburgh asserts the moral right to be identified as the author of this work in accordance with the Copyright, Designs and Patents Act 1988

This book is a work of non-fiction written in the form of a memoir. It is based on the author's personal experiences, reflections, and recollections. While every effort has been made to ensure accuracy, memory is inherently subjective, and some details may reflect the author's perspective or interpretation of events.

Isbn: 978-1-914399-24-4

This book is sold subject to the condition that it shall not be resold, lent, hired out or otherwise circulated without the express prior consent of the author.

Printed and bound by Ingram Spark
Cover Design © 2025 Mercat Design, images courtesy of Dreamstime. All Rights Reserved

Acknowledgements

I would like to dedicate My Perfect Companion: Because Love is Blind to those who were taken from us too soon and didn't get the opportunity to read my finished story. Mairi - a family relative. John - a volunteer for BASE and a dear friend. And to Ross- a volunteer and also a dear friend. And everyone else who passed away during writing, development and production of this book.

I would also like to thank my family and friends for their patience while I wrote and produced this book. They know and understand the commitment, time and dedication which went into writing my story. To my copy editor, Barbara Fotheringham who helped to correct my spelling, typos and grammar and amend proper English when required. To my additional editors, Palo Stickland, Pat Colville. And to Jenni Gudgeon who assisted with further edits, helping bring my book to life by including aspects of emotion and putting the finishing touches together. To my publisher, Sparsile Books Ltd for the final edits and creating the book design. To Lesley Wallace for the final proofread and spotting final little errors.

To the people mentioned in all of these places for their involvement, time and patience during the production of my book.

To all individuals named in my book, including My mum, my dad, my brother, my niece and nephew. And to all of my other family and to my closest friends. To all of the places and establishments mentioned in this book- especially in Anstruther and the surrounding area.

Without the inclusion of these places and establishments, I wouldn't have managed to complete my story.

PREFACE

Don't expect to rely on people to provide lifts to the East Sands Leisure Centre in St Andrews, nine miles from Anstruther, when transport isn't always available. I had started swimming in 2009 as this was the best way of keeping myself fit but that meant going several times a week. Unfortunately, I wasn't guaranteed a lift.

When no one was available to take me, I got the bus but the more I got the bus, the less I went. When I did go, I set targets—a few lengths to begin with, increasing to half a mile, then to a few lengths more and eventually a mile. The sound of the radio blasting out around the swimming pool got me through. Using the lane rope as a guide, I swam to the music—breaststroke after breaststroke, forcing my arms through the water and pulling them back, gliding my tired body through as I swam in time to One Republic's *Counting Stars*. My legs kicked feebly behind. Drained to exhaustion, I pulled myself out and collapsed on the tiles. I was seeing stars, never mind counting stars.

Don't expect to visit the cinema, and everything to remain the same when you have responsibilities. I have been a fan of movies most of my life, staying up to watch a late-night movie—something I shouldn't have done at eleven years old.

I was never a cinema-goer. There had been times my parents took my brother and me to blockbuster showings, such as *Jurassic Park* in 1992 and *Titanic* in 1997. That was when I could still see. However, things change and the emergence of audio description, introduced in the early 2000s, made it more accessible for a blind or partially sighted person to visit the cinema. Spectators are provided with a headset which connects to the screen via infrared capabilities, allowing them to hear the audio description, enjoying the film like other sighted viewers. The first time I experienced this service was in 2014 when a volunteer took me to see *Transcendence,* starring Johnny Depp , at the Odeon cinema in Dundee.

Don't expect one mobility training session to be enough to get around a town you haven't visited for years. In May 2014 I wanted a new venture, and a new challenge. I decided to test my abilities as a blind man and visit pubs somewhere else. St Andrews was a place I had been familiar with as a youngster but not so much in later life.

When you're blind, shops and pubs aren't easy to find, and some mobility training would be required. I called my local blind society to arrange this.

My mobility officer asked me to do the first leg on my own, which was a bus journey to St Andrews. I met her there. She asked me where I wanted to go. I had visited a few pubs prior to our training session but had to ask several passers-by for directions. I wanted to manage without asking anyone. I told her which ones I'd been to, and she instructed me how to get to them safely.

She showed me how to sweep my white stick in front, letting me know about landmarks I needed to be aware of. This pattern continued once a week for a month until I felt confident enough to go it alone.

Don't expect student volunteers to accompany you to the pub after a meal. Mum enjoyed swimming and had talked about going for a while, so she took me twice a week. As well as swimming on Tuesdays and Thursdays with Mum, I was also swimming on Fridays as part of a local charity for blind people, BASE (Blind, Activities, Support, Events).

Although this worked well, it was difficult to swim without bumping into other blind swimmers. Some students from the University of St Andrews were recruited to provide tandem swimming with the blind person, keeping them in line. Friday afternoons worked in my favour. At the end of some sessions, the swimmers and volunteer students went for a pizza. This meant I would stay in St Andrews and visit some pubs but, despite asking the students to accompany me, they rarely did.

Making my own way to The Cross Keys, the pub which would become my new 'local', I pulled myself onto a stool at the bar and began sipping on a cool foamy pint. They already knew what I drank and had started to refer to me as a 'local'.

I was aware of a man beside me but nearly an hour passed before either of us spoke. However, once we did, we blethered like we'd known each other for years. Russell became the first of my new friends. I enjoyed my trips to St Andrews for the peace and pizza.

Don't expect the cinema to be a regular thing when you're about to get a dog. Once I got into the audio description experience, I wanted to go every week. I enjoyed an animated movie or a fantasy fiction one, but most of all I loved horror films like *IT* or *The Conjuring*. The smell of popcorn, the taste of a sour bag of pick 'n' mix and the rumble of the surround sound experience was all too tempting. This was an experience I was hooked on. Although I struggled to see the large screen, cinemas now have all the home comforts like reclining seats, cup holders and places to put your food. On one occasion I felt so relaxed I drifted off to sleep listening to the audio description.

Don't expect to be captain of a pool team and don't assume you have to pick yourself to play. By January 2016, playing was getting harder as my sight deteriorated. I would have to give up playing the game I loved and still love. However, I had one goal before I retired from pool completely—to captain the team, which had finished bottom of the second division for the past fifteen years, and to prevent it from finishing bottom again. The irony was that I had re-joined the team I left in 2013. When The Royal Hotel was bought over and refurbished, the new owners wanted me as captain, but I declined, instead choosing to step up to play for a first-division team. At that time, I was improving. I was enjoying the game, potting balls and winning matches. 'Potting balls,' was a phrase I had become accustomed to during my spell in the topflight. The league chairman used to say, 'as long as you can pot balls, you'll win games.' Although this seems obvious, his words still run around my head today. In this league it wasn't so much potting as rarely missing that was the issue. After two-and-a-half seasons playing in the first division I re-joined the Royal as captain. I wanted to keep my existing players but needed them to improve. I also had to add to the squad, but most of all, I wanted to turn a team from a laughingstock into a team which was hard to beat. After that I would retire.

Don't expect to be a pool captain and be able to switch off. In my first half-season, I didn't have much to work with or the players to pick from; it was a tough start. My first full season in charge was different. I had players who wanted to sign for me. They had faith in me. I had something that previous captains before me didn't have. I held the team together. But togetherness was difficult to sustain. Soon I had more than a full squad turning up every week—a nice problem to have. Players had to be left out; something I knew all too well as I was left out of teams often enough when I played in the first division.

Who did we play next, who was available to play, what team should I pick, or more importantly, who would I leave out? I pondered these questions in the shower, watching television, lying in bed and even in the swimming pool. I remember calmly swimming along, then realising I was underwater. Panicking, I began flailing my arms about, trying to get back to the surface. I had fallen asleep while swimming. All because of pool. At the end of the season, we still finished bottom but with eight points, more than in any other recent season. It was a start, but I still had a goal to achieve.

Don't expect to rely on a volunteer to take you to the cinema in Dundee when you want to go all of the time, and they can't take you. It couldn't be too difficult for a blind man with crutches to make a fifty-mile round trip to the cinema on his own, could it? It was early October; we had won our first three pool matches of the season and my confidence was high. I decided to travel to the cinema alone. I took the opportunity to familiarise myself with apps on my iPhone. One was called Scot Talk, an app that could read out bus routes. It worked in several ways. It would highlight the nearest stop, which could be saved for later, and it could bring up a list of future stops, which I could also save. All I had to do was pick the stops I wanted and once on the bus, choose "track" and let voiceover announce the stops as the bus approached them.

I asked one of my players, who was from Dundee, which buses to get. I entered the stops he told me. Piece of cake I thought. Another app that was influential was Soundscape—a 3D map in your head. You simply open the app, put earphones in and a voice tells you what's around you. It also has a beacon feature which allows you to enter the destination, and the directions in your head lead you straight there. Four buses there and four buses back, and a bit of walking in between. Eight hours later I had successfully visited the cinema, watched a film and returned safely without any hiccups. Well, I'm being economical with the truth!

Don't expect to have a lifestyle like mine and not suffer the consequences. People assume that being born with cerebral palsy means I have a shorter life expectancy than most adults.

'How old are you now?' someone I knew asked me in a pub in 2018.

I told him. As if he didn't know! He hung around with my brother for years. His foamy pint was spilling over the side of his glass as his open mouth gave off a mixture of cannabis and bad breath.

'You've defied science then,' he said, composing himself, soaking up the froth, hiding the smell.

'What do you mean?' I asked.

He had obviously watched me struggle to pull myself onto the barstool.

'What's your life expectancy?'

'I'm no different from anyone else. Just because I have cerebral palsy doesn't mean to say I'm going to die earlier than you,' I told him, glowering at him over the rim of my pint.

My lifestyle wasn't healthy, but I was making the most of what I had left. I was going out too often and drinking too much. The recommended weekly intake for men and women in the UK is 14 units—equivalent to drinking no more than six pints of average-strength beer (4% ABV). I was drinking that amount per night!

If I didn't calm down, my life might be shorter than I expected. My weekend started on Thursday night. Monday night was pool practice and Wednesday was pool night— any excuse for a few pints. I had Sundays and Tuesdays off, allowing my body to recover slightly before starting again. I was enjoying the social side of pub life, but it was taking its toll and stumbling home was becoming difficult, so I started relying on taxis. My bank balance was taking a hit as well as my own balance.

Don't expect to step down as captain when you manage to finish the following season in mid-table. Yes, I did it. We finished fifth out of nine with fifteen points. But not everything was sunshine and roses. There were disappointed players. There were fall-outs between teams. Players left during the season. I offered to resign twice that season, but my team persuaded me to change my mind. After having eight pints one pool night, I pulled the whisky bottle out when I got home. I poured myself a large one, then another, then another. I was drinking myself into oblivion.

You can visit the cinema as many times as you like when you have volunteers to take you. Or now you are Mr Independent and go on your own now that you have the methods and capabilities to get you there. But don't expect this luxury to continue when you own a dog. Was this the end of visits to the cinema?

You can keep yourself fit by swimming regularly, but would Mum and I have to reduce how often we went? Mum enjoyed swimming as much as I did. Would we both have to stop?

You can be captain and achieve results no other captain of that pool team has managed in recent years. You can contemplate staying on for another season to carry on the success or try to better what you've already achieved by striving to get the team promoted to the first division. Believe me, the thought is tempting when your players want you to stay on to make the team become stronger—but emotional blackmail wasn't the answer. Was the answer to give up when I'd reached the heights I had? Did I have to give up?

You can drink five nights a week and enjoy drinking yourself into oblivion. You can enjoy the social aspect of going out, having a drink with your friends. I was making the most of what I had. My lifestyle wasn't healthy, but I enjoyed going out and meeting people.

Would all this have to stop when I got a dog?

Chapter 1

THE UNEXPECTED ANNOUNCEMENT

To be blind is not miserable; not to be able to bear blindness, that is miserable.

John Milton

It was October 2018. Mum's chin nearly hit the kitchen table when I asked her, 'How do you feel about becoming a granny again?' My brother, Michael, had two grown-up kids, Mya and Mikey, but I had no partner and hadn't even had any one-night stands… none that she was aware of, anyway.

'What you mean?' she asked.

'I would like a dog,' I replied.

The corners of her mouth rose, and her jaw-drop turned into a smile. I don't think Mum was expecting to be granny to a dog.

Dad stared through his glasses; his brown eyes magnified by the varifocal lenses. He stopped short as his vodka and Coke almost touched his lips, the ice chinking in the glass as he put it down firmly.

'Why not?' Mum continued, taking a sip of wine.

'How're you going to manage?' Dad probed, stroking the stubble on his chin.

I have glaucoma and cerebral palsy. I get around with two

elbow crutches. And in recent years have relied on a long cane—a white collapsible stick with a roller ball, to sweep the ground, to help guide me.

'We'll help him, Wullie,' Mum assured him.

I was surprised she supported the idea. Mum didn't like dogs. She had been bitten three times, twice by German Shepherds—I mean the dogs not sheep herders from Bavaria.

'Are you sure that's what you want?' Dad added. 'You know it'll be difficult.'

With my conditions, I knew owning a dog would be challenging. In fact, most people said it would be too difficult. A few months earlier, I'd had a conversation in a local pub with my best friend.

'I'm thinking about getting a dog,' I mumbled, midway through my fifth pint.

'Oh, right,' Stuart said, his focus on a football match on the large screen telly in front of us.

'Aye, I think it's time.'

'A guide dog?'

'No, I want a Jack Russell.'

'A rescue one?'

'No, a puppy.'

'I think you'll struggle with a Jack Russell. You're better with a Staffy or a rescue dog. It'll already be trained.'

'I realise that, Stuart, but I don't want a rescue dog,' I moaned, struggling with my pint. 'A rescue dog won't adapt to a disabled person. That's why I need to train a puppy from scratch, so it learns to adapt to my needs.'

'But a Jack Russell?' he said again, his attention on me

now. 'You're better with a Staffy, or a cat.'

He didn't take me seriously.

Mum, Dad and I continued our discussion at the kitchen table.

'I thought you didn't like dogs, Mum' I said.

'But I'll like yours,' she said, staring at me through her own varifocal lenses.

'It has to be a Jack then.'

'Whatever dog you think will be best for you,' she said, her bright red lips raised to her cheekbones.

I don't think Mum was aware of what Jack Russells are like. People are often dismissive of the breed. They say they bark. They bite. They chase and chew everything… To an extent, this is true. But is this not the case for most dogs? I was determined my dog would not do those things.

'Jack Russells need a lot of exercise,' Dad interjected.

'We'll walk it, Wullie. And he's got a niece and nephew who I'm sure will be willing to walk the dog,' Mum added.

I knew Jack Russells are energetic dogs and understood that perhaps this wasn't the best breed I could have chosen, but that's the one I had set my heart on.

'Dad, I need to know you're on board?'

'Aye, if that's what you want, we'll support you.'

'That's great,' I went on. 'It'll need to learn to walk with me. It'll be taught to do its business in the garden. And it'll not be given any titbits. Only dog food.'

'Aye, okay,' Dad said again.

'I want a boy, and a white one,' I added.

'It's like you have everything planned,' Dad said, raising

his glass to his lips.

'Why a white one?' Mum asked.

'A white Jack Russell will be easier to see,' I said.

Although I live with debilitating ailments, I am an independent thirty-seven-year-old man who has worked out how to overcome challenges, especially around the house.

Glaucoma has left me with a small degree of hazy vision, and distinguishing colours is problematic. However, I can differentiate contrasts of colour. In my kitchen, white cabinets stand out against black vinyl and in my living room, the walls are cream and the laminate walnut. A white Jack Russell would be ideal for me to see against my dark flooring. A white dog would also be easier to see out and about. Against the grass… against the concrete paths… a white one would be perfect.

I may have little balance, but I have a strong upper body and get around using the furniture. I would have to learn new skills…to move quicker…and to be wiser. Despite my poor balance, I would also have to learn how to carry a puppy.

But most people seemed to think getting a Jack Russell was a bad idea. I had so many disheartening comments. I was so fed up with all the negativity, I stopped talking about dogs to anybody outside my immediate family. I still had the support and encouragement from my mum and dad. They gave me renewed vigour. Therefore, I decided I would go for it.

I began to search for a dog the minute Mum and Dad supported the idea. A few people were selling Jack Russells on Gumtree—most of them from Dundee. I found a male dog called Patrick. But he was three. I saved the owner's details with the intention of contacting him, but I never made that call because I had made it clear that I wanted a puppy. Therefore, the search continued. There was an elderly Jack Russell from a re-homing centre in mid-Lothian. But he was a rescue dog who was on his last legs. Dad had also found the same dog. If I really wanted a Jack Russell, it had to be from a proper breeder. Breeders who bred Jack Russells were difficult to come by.

Nothing had been mentioned for months, and I hit a dead end. I lost all hope. But fortunes changed in mid-August 2019 when friends sourced a Jack Russell breeder from West Lothian. It was the breed I wanted. It was the proper colouring. And it was a male. I finally found the Jack Russell puppy I wanted. I planned to call my dog Dobby if it was a boy or, if I couldn't find a boy, it would be Luna: both characters from the Harry Potter books.

Chapter 2

THE NIGHT BEFORE

It was Wednesday 4th September 2019, the first pool night of the new season. My players threatened to leave during the summer if I didn't remain as captain. I stayed on but in three days' time I was due to pick up Dobby.

The East Neuk Pool League is a winter pool league that was formed in the early eighties. The purpose of this competition was to break up the week by getting people out on a Wednesday night. Teams compete against each other in venues along the East Neuk of Fife as far as St Andrews over thirty-two weeks. Every team has eight players and can have up to four reserves. They play eight singles games and four doubles games.

Our first match was away to the Balcomie in Crail, which was a venue where we often struggled because they had a consistency of players who had played together for years and were better than us. But I was confident with the squad I had formed.

Plenty of players were turning up every week, so we had a good chance. I dictated the line up to a teammate, who wrote the names on the sheet. The opposing captain and I shook hands, and the match commenced.

The first game got underway. Stuart was playing against one of our friends. As the game played out, my player who filled in the sheet wobbled over and placed a pint in front of me. Some teams were not as helpful as the Royal. They made sure my glass was never empty.

'Thanks, Ali,' I said, taking a sip.

'I don't think Big Al's going to play this season,' he said, sitting beside me.

The bench shrieked in protest as the padded cushions sank a few inches.

'He says that every season,' I replied, avoiding his gaze.

I knew where this conversation was heading.

'What about making someone else vice-captain? Someone who'll be available every week.'

I smelled little puffs of dust when players thumped their cues on the carpet. An outburst of cheers and clapping echoed around the pool room. Stuart had won. I can often follow the game with my ears, sensing whose shot it was. Going by the crowd's reactions and the clunk of balls dropping down the holes into the chute, I knew how each game went without being able to see what was happening. But it was difficult when a player was talking to me when I was trying to concentrate.

'What about me?' Ali asked.

After tonight, I wouldn't care who was vice-captain. Or would I? Walking away from the team I built; I wanted someone capable of running it. But was he that person?

'I suppose I could make you vice-captain,' I said, not

paying him much attention. I was too busy focusing on who I'd picked next.

'I won't let you down,' he said, holding out his hand.

More cheers, a bigger roar, and we were two games up.

His little round face turned as bright as the red pool balls on the table.

Half time came and the sandwiches arrived. We were five-three up and with four doubles games to go. I was confident we could start the season with a win. I looked forward to half time. It meant, as well as scoffing wonderful food, I could soak up the pints, so I could manage more.

'What's wrong, Billy?' Stuart asked, as he sank into the recently vacated bench.

I hadn't yet told any of my players that I was getting a dog. I had a team of good players, but my mind wandered, excited, but nervous about getting my puppy. I had no idea what it'd be like and if the first pool match of the season would be my last. I didn't want to let my team down by announcing this information.

'I'm getting my dog.'

'Thought you weren't your usual self.'

'My mind's on Saturday.'

'You're definitely getting one this time?'

'Aye, but I don't want anybody in the team knowing,' I said, chewing on an egg sandwich. 'This will have to stop. I'll not be able to captain the team anymore, at least for away games.'

'I see,' he said, reaching for his own sandwich.

The Royal won nine-three. We'd just pulled off an excellent victory—the first in years against them. I peered over the rim of my empty pint glass, a wide grin on my face while my team cheered and roared with the impressive win. If that was to be my last involvement, at least I was going out on a high. The grin faded as my thoughts returned to Saturday. I selected a bottle of Glenkinchie from the cupboard when I got home. I poured myself a large measure and celebrated both winning and looked forward to getting my first dog.

TWELVE DAYS BEFORE DOBBY

I swung my legs out of bed on the morning of the 26th of August 2019. It was the day my life was going to change forever, when I reached for my mobile on the bedside table. I opened WhatsApp and noticed I had several missed messages and calls. 'Not everyone's up at the crack of dawn,' I muttered, using the voiceover function to listen to the first of the messages which had been sent three hours earlier. The first few messages had been deleted and those that remained were difficult to decipher. I skipped to the next, and the next. With increasing anxiety, my finger rested on the last message. My chin could have broken the display screen as I listened.

'The puppy is ill! Money back!' the last message said.

Unwilling to leave it there, I selected the number and phoned the breeder.

'What do you mean puppy is ill?' I asked, my bottom lip quivering.

'I can't sell you him,' she replied. 'His heart isn't right.'

'There was nothing wrong when I viewed him last week,' I mumbled, trying to disguise the tremor in my voice.

I wasn't buying her story. Everything was moving so well.

Why the sudden change of heart? Perhaps she could have been to the vet before I called her back. Could it be that she changed her mind and concocted a convincing excuse?

Resigned to the fact I wasn't getting him, I hung up and phoned Mum and Dad, who were on the train home from Aberdeen. Although Mum didn't like dogs, she and Dad were looking forward to taking me to pick Dobby up. They knew by the sound of my voice that I was holding back tears.

'Don't worry about it, Billy,' Dad said. 'There'll be other dogs.'

'But I wanted that one.'

'I know you did, but there's nothing we can do about it,' Dad assured me.

'Keep your chin up,' Mum added.

THREE DAYS LATER

I was on my way home from one of my blind group events. It must have been quite a long trip because we were on a coach, and we only used coaches for longer journeys. My phone pinged. It was a WhatsApp tone. I picked it up and read the message. It was her! What did she want this time?

'Hi,' it said.

I put the phone down on the seat beside me. But it pinged again.

'How are you?' the message said this time. But this time, I replied.

'How do you think I am?' I wrote back. 'I thought I was getting a dog!'

'I've still got him if you want him,' she said.

'Of course I want him,' I replied. 'But you'll have to let me talk to Mum and Dad first.'

'Okay,' she finished.

Mum, Dad and I sat around the table that same night.

'Why the sudden change of heart?' Dad queried, resting his fork on his plate.

'I don't know,' I replied, picking up my cup of tea.

'She was happy to sell you him before,' Mum added.

'I don't know. I didn't think she was sure when we went to view him. It may be because of the nature of my disabilities.'

'I think it's because she had him reserved for someone else,' Dad offered.

'Dobby's testicles hadn't dropped, and I think the person didn't take him for that reason.'

'What are you thinking, Billy?' Mum probed.

'I'm not sure if I want to take a dog from her if she keeps lying to us. First it was a murmur in his heart and now she's happy to sell him to me.'

'One of my customers said dogs get murmurs in their hearts and they live a full life,' Dad said.

'Aye, but I don't think he's got anything wrong with his heart,' I interrupted. 'I just don't think she thought I was capable of raising a dog.'

'It's up to you,' Mum said.

'Aye, I had my heart set on him.'

'Do you want to let her know you want him then?'

'No, I don't want anything more to do with the woman,'

'You want me to phone her?' Mum offered.

'Aye, okay then.'

Mum had a lengthy conversation with her, and it was arranged that we would collect him the following Saturday.

We believe that she thought that I was going to permanently keep my dog in a cage and that's why she didn't want to sell him to me. But that was never going to happen. However, she changed her mind, and a little later than planned, we were off to collect him on the 7th of September.

THE NIGHT BEFORE

I pulled myself onto the barstool in The Anstruther Boat House—the same pub in which my brother's friend, smelling of cannabis and bad breath, spoke to me a year earlier, suggesting I'd defied science. It was my last Friday night out before we collected Dobby the following day. Where the man had previously sat was another couple, regular weekend drinkers who knew me, but despite having talked with them several times, I didn't know their names.

'How are you?' the man to my left asked.

'Yeah, I'm good thanks,' I replied, trying to balance my crutches and long cane against the bar.

'I've not seen you for a few weeks,' he continued, attracting a staff member to serve me.

'The usual?' the barman asked.

'Aye, please.' I turned to the couple. 'It's probably the last time you'll see me for a while.'

'Oh, why's that?'

'I'm getting a dog tomorrow,' I explained, picking up my freshly delivered pint.

'What kind of dog are you getting?'

'A Jack Russell.'

'Oh, they're great family dogs,' he said turning to his wife. 'Your mum had a Jack Russell, didn't she?'

'Yes, she did,' she said.

'Aye, I've heard that about them,' I said. 'I've never had a dog before, but I thought it was time,' I went on, taking a large sip of my pint.

'They are very loyal little things,' he continued. 'My mother-in-law's Jack Russell fetched things for her.'

'I didn't think they did things like that,' I replied.

'Oh yeah, they'll bring your slippers to you. They'll fetch you your mail. Her mum,' he went on, glancing to his wife again, 'she can leave pizza on the coffee table, and it'll still be there in the morning.'

'I hope my dog does all those things,' I said.

I had two pints while chatting to the couple before I left for my next pub. They were a lovely pair to talk to. I believe they only stay in Anstruther for a few weeks in the summer months, and so I thought that would be the last time I spoke to them. Thanking them for their company, I gathered up my crutches and long cane to leave.

'I hope everything goes well with your dog,' the man finished.

'I hope so too,' I called back, exiting the pub.

I rarely used my long cane because it's difficult to use with crutches. However, I was taught to hold the top of the cane with my thumb and forefinger. By gripping my hand at the edge of my crutch handle, I can sweep my long cane in front of me. I started to rely on it more. My sight had been deteriorating for about twenty years, and although I am familiar with Anstruther, I began to feel safer using it. Without it, if someone didn't know me, they would just think I was disabled. When I use it, they realise I also have sight problems. It is especially handy on a bus because there people are more willing to assist. How would I manage my long cane with a dog? I would worry about that later.

~~~

I swept my way along the shore and arrived at the Royal about five minutes later. The pub was busy as usual, and I made my way to my normal spot at the end of the bar where I sat when I captained the pool team. But sometimes it was too busy to sit there, so someone would guide me to another seat or give up their one.

The Royal and the Bank often had live music at the weekend, and the Royal had a karaoke. It would be my last chance for a song or two. I requested my usual, *Folsom Prison Blues* and *Teenage Kicks*—two songs I was used to performing and had learned the words to. The Royal was full of regulars and many of them spoke to me. But I didn't want to make a fuss about getting a dog the next day, so after three pints, I made my way to the Bank.

I heard the music booming from the Bank as soon as I left the Royal. The high ceilings in the Bank make it difficult for me to hear someone if it's busy. And if it's busy, it's also loud. I managed three pints before my taxi home, but visiting the toilet was difficult because I had to avoid speakers placed in the middle of the floor. Passing the speakers was ear splitting.
~~~

My long cane was my eyes and ears. The floor was slippery on the way to the toilet and my crutches went from under me. A slippery surface is something my long cane cannot detect, so I fell flat on my face. Not a good sign the night before I got my dog! Was I going to fall with him? No one witnessed the fall, so I kept it to myself. When I returned to finish my pint before my taxi, the couple from The Anstruther Boat House stood at the bar. They wished me all the best again and I headed for the door.

I had one last look at the pub before my taxi driver helped me into his minibus and took me up the road.

'This is it then, Eddie. I don't know when I'll see you again.'

'No problem, Billy. You look after that dog of yours when you get him tomorrow,' he replied. 'What are you calling him again?'

'Dobby.'

'Oh, yeah, from *Harry Potter.*'

'Aye, that's it.'

Eddie helped me from his taxi and he, like a lot of people that night, wished me all the best. I stepped into an empty house but for the first time in thirteen years, I was going to have company the following evening. Despite having sunk several pints, I almost skipped towards my bed.

Chapter 3

OUR FIRST NIGHT

I planned to phase Dobby in, one room, at a time when I got him home, but I let him into the living room with me on the first night. The idea of owning a dog was for the company and so I wanted him beside me while I watched telly. He pottered about the living room before he stood on his little outstretched back legs with his paws on the couch. Lowering myself to my knees, I placed my forearm under his bum, my other hand on his breastbone and gently eased him onto the couch.

My fingers gently glided through his soft, furry body as I stroked him. He had a puppy fresh smell as I buried my head into his fluffy coat before gently placing a tender kiss on the top of his head while he lay contented beside me. Never in a million years did I think the moment would arrive that I would be in my house with a dog of my own.

When it was time for bed, I bundled him under my right forearm. Holding my hand under the top of his chest, I used my left hand to grip the furniture. Carefully, I lifted him and carried him to his cage in the kitchen. I lowered him in, stroked his head before closing the door. I would have preferred to take him through to my bedroom rather than putting him in a cage, but it was too soon. Besides, what would my dad say if he found us curled up on the big bed together?

Moving into the living room, I passed my echo device and had an idea. Not knowing if it would work, I asked, 'Alexa, play Forth One to wake me in the morning. To my surprise she said, 'For what time?'

'Six o'clock,' I told her.

'Would you like it for the same time every morning?' she offered.

'Yes,' I said.

At least I had no chance of sleeping in.

~~~

'What time do you get up in the morning?' the breeder had asked me when we collected Dobby from Livingston.

I was reluctant to tell her I got up about lunch time. Those days were a thing of the past now. Getting up early was going to be a shock to my system and having a puppy was going to change my life in so many ways.

'Depends,' I said.

'I feed all my dogs at six.'

Six o'clock in the morning, I thought. The last time I saw 6 am, my mate was pushing me home from the pub in a wheelie bin after a lock-in.

'I get up around that time,' I lied.

'You can feed him a bit later if you want.'

'If that's when he's being fed, I'll feed him then.'
~~~

<center>~~~</center>

I drew the living room curtains before I went to bed. Something began to seep through my sock before reaching the left-hand one. The substance warmed the sole of my foot. My nostrils were filled with the smell of recently laid dog shit as I bent down to investigate. My left sock was caked in Dobby's poop. With my sense of smell, I was surprised I hadn't noticed. I was in over my head. The breeder might have toilet trained Dobby, but I had a long, bumpy road ahead of me and he was going to need retraining from scratch. Fishing my mobile from my pocket, I phoned Dad.

'He's not just pooped, Billy,' Dad announced, his arms limp by his sides.

'He's not?' I threw my shit-covered socks in the bathroom, having managed to slide my way along the floor without making any more mess.

'He's done a pee. How did he get through?'

'I let him.'

'You'll have to stick to the kitchen!'

Confining Dobby to the one room wouldn't be practical. My kitchen was fairly spacious, but his cage was big and took up a lot of floor space. I had to make do. Or did I?

'But…' I continued.

'But no. It's too early to let him in the living room with you. Good job I didn't take him into my room.

'What were you doing with him?'

'Watching telly. I had him on the couch, cuddled up beside me. I was telling him he was a good boy.'

'Well, he'll think peeing and pooping on the floor is the

right thing to do now.'

Dad cleaned up the accidents—because, after all, they were only accidents. The house shook as he left, letting the back door slam behind him while I scrubbed my feet.

I was naive to think getting a dog would be simple. I expected everything to be instant when I got him home.

~~~

I was wakened, not by my radio, but to the sound of whining. I pushed the chime on my talking watch and it announced 4.03. It was far too early to get up. The whining stopped so I rolled over. The whining began again—a little louder. Not wanting to leave him crying, I went through to comfort him. Lowering myself to my knees, I fumbled for the two bolts, slid them across and opened the door. Reaching my hand inside, I located his small head and gave it a rub. Then I fingered my bunch of keyrings before finding the back door key. The door was barely open when he went running out, but he was only out for five minutes when he came back in. I gathered him up, cuddled him to my neck, allowing his little whiskers to tickle my chin before I placed him gently back in his cage.

'No more crying, Dobby,' I said, stroking his little head. 'We'll show everyone we can do this, pal. Dad will let you out again in a wee while.' I closed his door.

~~~

I was standing in a crowd of thousands of screaming fans, their hands waving in the air. A woman beside me tore her top off and threw it towards the stage. Shocked at the sight of this topless girl, I focused my attention on the singer who was yelling into the microphone. My head was about to explode. Over the screaming voices, I called, 'I know you're a good singer, but would you shut the fuck up?' Not hearing me over the screams of revellers, he sung on regardless.

Alexa had done her job. The radio station Forth One had wakened me but it took me a few minutes to understand what was happening. Lewis Capaldi hadn't been singing to a crowd of people, his song was playing on the radio, blasting from my echo device. Realising the music was just on the other side of the wall from Dobby, I swung my legs out of bed, threw on my T-shirt from the previous day and hurried through.

As I approached the kitchen, he became alert and began leaping around his cage. He must have heard me even over the music. Or learned my smell already. I told Alexa, 'STOP', and the music stopped. Mum and Dad's neighbour suggested we put a blanket over Dobby's cage so he would think it was still dark. The blanket also added warmth, making it like a little den. However, I had decided to leave the front uncovered. I opened his cage before opening the back door. I listened to the pit patter of small paws pad across the kitchen floor behind me and then felt his soft hair brush my left ankle as he went out. I sat on the back step to have a cigarette while he was outside. However, enticing him back inside was not easy. I couldn't see him. Dad promised me that the fence was sound. But how could I know? Dobby was so small; he might have been able to squeeze his body under the fence.

'Dobby, Dobby,' I called.

As much as I tried, he wouldn't come in. I prepared his

food while he was outside.

'Dobby, Dobby, come and get your breakfast, pal,' I tried again moving his food around his bowl to encourage him.

I was relieved to hear his tiny paws pad across the floor again. He nibbled at some of it and walked away. Running my finger around his bowl, I could tell he had eaten most of his dry food and not much wet. I planned on only giving him dry food; that's what a friend gave his Jack Russell. I decided to give it a few days to see what happened. After his breakfast, I played with him for a while, I rough-and-tumbled, rolling him on his back. Dobby was throwing his legs in the air, he just didn't care, like he was a baby getting its nappy changed. His head moved from side-to-side, his jaws opening and shutting like he was trying to catch a fly but the only thing he was catching was my fingers. His paws pushed against my hands as I tried to tickle his belly.

It took me nearly an hour; let Dobby out, feed him and play with him, and I was preparing to put him back in his cage when Dad appeared in the kitchen.

'How was he after last night's escapade?' he asked.

'Aye, he was fine. He had a couple whines through the night but nothing major.'

'That's good then.'

'I was up at four though. I didn't want to leave him, so I went through and comforted him.'

'You shouldn't do that,' Dad interjected.

'Why not?'

'He needs to learn, when you come through, that's when he's allowed out. I have customers who've told me that.'

Every reply under the sun swam around my head, but I didn't have the response. Dad meant well and was only trying to help.

'Give me a break, Dad. I'm trying my best.'

'Well, you knew owning a dog was going to be hard,' Dad continued. 'He's peed on the floor in front of his cage.'

'Ah shit, I thought I let him out in time.'

'Did you open the back door first?'

My face reddened. I clenched both fists, my nails pressing into my palms.

'No, I opened his door first,' I said.

'Always open the back door first.'

'That's easier said than done when he's banging his head into the cage door trying to get out.'

He rested his large hand on my shoulder.

'Open the back door first, then let him out. He'll learn that's how it works.'

The idea of getting Dobby home on the Saturday was that Mum and Dad would be around to help. Dad was off work Saturday to Monday and Mum was always on hand. After my first night, I was shattered so I tried a lie down.

~~~

'I give him a quarter tin of Pedigree Chum and a scoop of his biscuits with each meal four times a day,' the breeder explained, the day we collected Dobby.

There's one thing I've learned in life! Some people don't know how to interact with a disabled person. She was explaining everything to Dad as if I wasn't in the room. Countless
~~~

times I have said, 'I can talk for myself, thank you.' Sometimes it worked. Sometimes it didn't.

'Can you email me the paperwork that you just gave to Dad so I can read it for myself?' I asked.

'Yeah, I'll do that for you,' she said, with a hint of reluctance in her voice, but focused on me this time.

'Thank you,' I said, knowing I would never receive the email.

'If he eats his biscuits, he will never have diarrhoea,' she continued, holding up a bag. 'He may get fed up with the same stuff so break up some ham or cold meat and mix that with his food.'

She gave us some extras to take away: three tins of wet food, a bag of dry food and some toys. My head was in a whirl. I just wanted to escape from the woman's abruptness.

Mum checked the folder that his breeder had given us when we arrived home. His paperwork included a chart stating daily feeding times and amounts. It was handy as I'd never had a dog. She provided dates for wormer, flea and tick tablets. We pinned these to the inside of the cupboard door, which was now Dobby's cupboard. I wanted my dog to be healthy, so I stuck to her instructions.

I also needed to know how to prepare Dobby's food. So standing at the kitchen sink, Mum talked me through the process.

'Hold out your hand, palm up,' she instructed.

She placed a can on my outstretched fingers.

'They've got ring pull tops like beans.'

'Okay,' I said, folding the ring back and pulling the lid off.

It was as easy as opening a can of Coke.

'Take the spoon and dig it inside.'

'How much do I need?' I asked, withdrawing a spoonful.

'That's enough. Put that in his bowl and add another two,' she said, studying the meat on the spoon. Now, use this cup and take some stuff out of that bag and add it to the bowl.'

I felt something was missing!

'What about his biscuits?'

'What biscuits? That's all that's there.'

'His breeder said something about biscuits.'

Dad was tidying the garden.

'Wullie, where's Dobby's biscuits?' she asked, calling to him through the open window.

'What?' he called back in his typical way.

Dad is quite deaf, so we always have to repeat what we say to him.

She asked again, a little louder this time.

He came in and looked over the instructions like he was assembling flat-packed furniture.

'I'm not sure,' he said, consulting the paperwork. 'That's all that's here.'

'What d'you mean you don't know?' I queried.

'There's just the cans and a bag of pellets. There's another bag but that's just extra pellets. I don't see any biscuits.'

'His breeder insisted I give him biscuits…'

'Aye, aye, I'll look online for them,' he said, stepping outside again.

'I knew you should have gone in with us, Mum,' I said, emptying the dry pellets over his wet food. 'How do I know when it's enough?'

'You'll know when the bowl is full.'

I did as she said and laid my hand on top of the bowl. It was just more than level. I can't stand without leaning against or holding onto something. Transferring Dobby's food from the worktop to the floor was tricky. To overcome this, I knelt on the floor using the furniture by placing one hand on a chair and the other on the worktop. I lost my balance if I wasn't set before I let go. I was then able to reach up and retrieve his bowl. I moved it to the chair before finally placing it on the floor in front of his cage. The same process was carried out for Dobby's water bowl.

'You'll have to keep that spoon separate. That's Dobby's spoon now,' Mum said.

'What d'you mean keep it separate?'

'You'll not be able to use that now you've used it for Dobby's food.'

'Why not? I'll wash it like all the rest of the dishes, and it'll be fine.'

It didn't matter if I used Dobby's spoon. I washed it with the rest of the dishes, dried and put it away. Preparing Dobby's food was simple enough. Knowing I would manage on my own, Mum and Dad left for the night.

Chapter 4

A REALITY CHECK

We were away to St Monans Bowling Club for our next pool match the following Wednesday. I had decided not to go but left it as long as possible before telling my new vice-captain. I visited the kitchen to check on Dobby, opening the cage door to encourage him out but he was happy, curled up in his bed. He was usually settled by half past six. This was a bit early for him because if he didn't go out to do the toilet that was him until six o'clock next morning. I watched television while I waited until seven thirty. I sent my apologies by text message. I had no intentions of going. It was my first Wednesday night off from pool in years and I looked forward to a night in with Dobby.

'I'm sorry, I'm not going to make it,' I said.

I needed an excuse to why I couldn't make it, so I told him that I hadn't been able to settle Dobby. But he was tucked up in his cage. The team now knew I had a dog and that I might not make many away games.

'So, I'll be taking charge tonight?' the vice-captain's message said.

I don't think he expected to be in charge so soon after

being made vice, but he didn't know at the time that I was getting a dog. He should have been delighted to take the team.

'Well, you wanted the job,'

'Okay,' he replied. 'No problem.'

I was off the hook. I had a free night. A free night to enjoy time with Dobby if he ever decided to venture out. He wouldn't budge so I closed his cage and went to bed early.

~~~

I went to Mum's for tea at least four times a week before I got Dobby, and this arrangement didn't have to change.

'What will you do with Dobby when you're here for tea?' Mum asked.

'He'll come here,' Dad said.

Mum's face drooped and her cheeks turned a deep shade of purple.

My vocal cords seemed to have jammed, but I managed a squeaky, 'We can't leave him.'

'Aye, that'll be fine,' she said. 'I never thought about that. And what about his tea?' she continued.

'We'll bring it down,' Dad said.

'Will that not be a bit of a clart?' she asked.

'Not really. I'll bag it up.'

'Okay then.'

The first time Dobby was at Mum and Dad's was the Friday after getting him. Normally I got a taxi to the pub after tea before getting Dobby, but it was a walk straight home this time. I followed behind Dad while he walked in front with Dobby. I know my own way home, but I'm used to walking
~~~

behind Dad. I bought a retractable lead for when I would be able to walk Dobby. It was supposed to be for my use only, allowing me to extend or retract the lead close or far enough from my crutches. But Dad was using it. I am not able to use a short, handheld lead. Everyone else had to use the short lead when walking Dobby. My purpose of owning an extendable lead was not to allow the lead to retract in and out, but to close the clip when I thought Dobby was a safe distance from my crutches. Dad was using it for the wrong reason.

Dad made sure Dobby was settled in his cage when we got home before leaving us to it. My talking watch announced 19:23. Could I do it?

I contemplated for some time, glancing towards Dobby's cage where he was tucked up. The next bus was 20:03, and I was running out of cigarettes. I could kill two birds with one stone—catch the bus, get off across from the shop, get my cigarettes, have two pints in the Royal, and get the 22:28 bus home. I decided at five to eight that's what I'd do.

'How's your dog?' a friend asked outside the shop.

I told him he was fine.

'How's the dog?' asked the woman behind the counter.

'He's fine,' I said again.

I headed to the Royal, ordered a Fosters and sat on a barstool.

'How's the wee dog?' the woman next to me asked.

'Aye, he's fine,' I replied, enjoying the ice-cold sensation of a fresh pint touch my dry, parched lips.

I was telling these people he was fine but how did I know? He was on his own. I didn't want to leave him, but sometimes you need to. Guilt riddled my thoughts as I held my pint. I know it was too soon to leave him on his own, but he would get used to it and I wouldn't make a habit of it. I was missing the little hairy thing already.

'That's good,' she said. 'What about toilet training?'

'He's good for his age.'

'That's really good,' she went on. 'It takes a while to toilet train puppies.'

'Aye, I thought that, too.'

The barmaid butted in.

'Out for cigarettes, are you?' she said with a smile.

'Aye,' I said, lifting my head towards her.

'You can't be out as long now you have a dog.'

'No, I can't,' I said. 'Only two pints, then up the road.'

True to my word, I went for the 22:28 bus.

I opened Dobby's cage door when I got home, reached in and gave his soft head a rub.

He'd been on his own for two-and-a-half hours, so I tried to encourage him out, but he didn't move. He would at least need to go out for the toilet. I had left the back door open for him. Instead, he turned around and faced the wall.

'I'm sorry, Dobby, but you have to get used to being on your own sometimes' I said, stroking his head and neck. 'It'll not be very often, and I'll always come home to you, pal, I promise.'

I had a strong urge to lift him out of his cage and carry him through to my room, but it was too early for that. Disappointed, I closed his cage door and went to bed.

Confining Dobby to one room was difficult. I'd had him

for one week, but each day was a challenge. I watched his every move, but he was into everything. It was the morning of Saturday 14th. Running my hand where his snout had been, I found a rupture on the door threshold—a chewed splinter of wood that became bigger every time Dobby had another try. The corner of the wall had little teeth marks where he'd found somewhere new. Dogs can be homewreckers if owners don't tackle the problem early. I didn't want to be one of those people with an out-of-control Jack Russell. I picked him up and held him close, gently telling him chewing things was wrong but when he persisted, I put him in his cage. Taking the opportunity for some respite, I lay down. I'd barely done so when the back door opened. The cage rattling sounded like a possessed gorilla trying to escape from the zoo when his granny and grandad arrived.

'What's he doing in his cage?' Dad asked.

'I've just put him in,' I shouted, swinging my legs out of bed and sitting up.

'But why's he in his cage?' he called back.

'I told you, Dad. I had to put him in,' I said, shuffling my way through. 'He was chewing everything. I couldn't leave him out of his cage so he could destroy the kitchen. That's my way of dealing with it,' I said, running my fingers through my hair."

'What's he chewing?' Dad asked, scanning for tell-tale signs.

I showed them where he was targeting.

Jean Donaldson, in her book *The Culture Clash*, states that 'There was a time when chewing in domestic dogs was viewed as either a stage that "teething" puppies went through or else a sign of a neurotic, screwed up dog. Now we know better. Chewing is a normal canine pastime that is both enjoyable for the dog and keeps the jaws and teeth in good shape.' On the other hand, in her book about Jack Russells, Carry Aylward says '…if he's not play biting, he is probably chewing something, which is natural because he is teething.'

'Your brother's a joiner, he'll fix that,' Mum said, studying the splintered wood.

'He'll grow out of that,' Dad added.

'He might not, he's a Jack Russell,' I said. 'I've lived here thirteen years and as far as I'm concerned, it is my house, but it belongs to the council. I can't have chunks out of walls.'

Jean Donaldson also says, 'Remember, dogs have no concept of things in your house being "worth" anything apart from their obvious suitability as chew objects. They also have no concept of right and wrong, only safe and dangerous.'

'I'll need to do something about it,' I groaned.

Carry Aylward suggests the answer is to, '…keep an abundant supply of toys and treats at hand—lots of things he IS allowed to chew on,' and Donaldson agrees when she says, 'Dogs get into chew toys the way humans get into spy novels or an absorbing movie. The problem is simply one of choice of chew object: we would like the dog to discriminate between dog chew toys and all the other items in the house.'

Dad told me to have plenty chew toys. The thing was, I did, but I never had them to hand.

Between September 7th and 13th, Mum went shopping in Dundee. Anticipating evenings with Dobby in his cage and me with nights to myself, I asked her to pick up a few Blu-rays from HMV. I needed something to pass the time. Mum was good at checking if a film had audio description, so I gave her a list. I had seen *Split,* and the recent sequel, *Glass,* but hadn't seen the first of the trilogy *Unbreakable.* I also asked her to pick me up *Pet Sematary* and *Halloween, 2018.*

Whilst watching *Unbreakable,* I made several trips to the kitchen to re-fill my glass with whisky and lemonade, trying not to disturb Dobby. I made three extra trips: on the first I took the whisky bottle to the living room, then some cans of lemonade, and finally, my glass. Usually, I smoked out the back but instead used the front door. However, I had my last cigarette of the evening at the back door. I thought if I opened Dobby's cage door and sat on the doorstep, he might come out. But he didn't. I tempted him with a toy, but he wouldn't budge. Squeaking the toy managed some movement from him, but he showed little interest and turned away again. He would at least need the toilet, so I tried to usher him to the door. But he didn't move. Resigned, I closed both doors and went to bed. What was the point of having a dog if he didn't do anything!

~~~

The third pool fixture was on Wednesday 18th September, our first home match against St Andrews University B—a team I was confident we would beat. They tend to finish bottom of the league each season, which used to be us. Dad popped in on his way home from work to check on us.

Hesitantly I asked, 'Can you run me to the Royal, please?'
~~~

'Aye,' he said. 'What time?'

I recognised a reluctance in his response. He knew what time; he took me down for most games. He felt that I shouldn't be going out at all. I no longer had a social life. But that was my fault for getting a dog. But a little mixing with friends wouldn't hurt.

'Seven thirty,' I confirmed.

'Okay, I'll be up for you then,' he said, closing the door.

I had an hour and a half. Time to make tea. Time to prepare Dobby's tea. Maybe time to play with him. Ten minutes before Dad arrived, I tried to settle Dobby in his cage. He was at the wall again. I moved him away. He went back. I repeated the act. He did it again. Frustrated, I pulled his collar. I wished I hadn't. He yelped.

'Aw, I'm sorry wee man,' I said, picking him up and holding him to my chest. 'I didn't mean to hurt you.' I ran my hand gently down his back.

Perhaps it was too difficult and raising a puppy was a lot harder than I expected.

I placed him in his cage as Dad arrived.

'You need to get your priorities right,' Dad said on our way to the van.

'What d'you mean?'

'You can't be running a pool team now you have a dog,' he barked.

'I know, Dad,' I said. 'I've been trying to give up for a while, but they won't let me.'

'You're going to have to tell them.'

'It's hard,' I continued.

'If you're not coping, you need to say now so we can give Dobby up to another home.'

'That's not what I meant.'

None of us wanted to give him up, and that was never going to happen. I had decisions to make. The only way I was going to make it work was to give up pool and other enjoyments in my life for a while and spend some quality time with Dobby.

'If you like, me and your mum could train him for you,' Dad offered.

'No!'

'You don't have to walk him, we can.'

'That's not why I got a dog. He'll respond to you more than me.'

We had agreed before I got him that I would train him and that he would learn to walk with me. And that's what I was determined to do.

'He's your dog. He lives with you. He'll still be your buddy if we walk him for you,' Dad said.

'Right, I'll pick the team, tell them I'm done and be home in half-an-hour.'

The barmaid announced, 'Here's your captain now,' as I walked through the doors of the Royal. It was like I entered an empty room. I sensed twenty pairs of eyes focused on me as I made my way to my usual stool at the end of the bar where I could keep an eye on things. I'd cut it fine.

'I didn't think you were coming,' Big Al said. 'I already picked the team.'

Incidentally, my new vice-captain only lasted one match,

after a 9-3 loss.

'I had things to sort out,' I said, slouching in my seat.

'Tell me your line-up and I'll rewrite the sheet,' he said.

'I'm out!'

'What d'you mean?' he said, picking up his pen.

'I can't do it anymore. I've got a dog. He is my priority. I can't leave him on his own.'

'Okay, I'll take over, then.' He wrote the last name on a new sheet.

He had played for me long enough to predict my line-up. He probably had it my way to begin with.

That was easier than I expected. It was a big weight lifted from my shoulders. It was sad to let my team go, but I had done it for the right reasons. I had Dobby to concentrate on instead.

I had one pint because I told Dad I would be half-an-hour. The player picked to play second ran me home, which gave me enough time to drink my pint while he played his game and have me home within the half hour. I left the Royal with mixed emotions, never to return as captain. Before I left, I encouraged all my team to play for the new captain and not move to other teams. It was out of my hands. They could do what they liked. Whatever happened, my heart was still with the Royal, and its players.

A light was on in my house, which meant Dad had gone back to dog-sit. I walked in to find him holding my puppy.

'I've done it, Dad,' I said. 'I've given up.'

'It's for the best,' he said, stroking Dobby's head.

'I know.'

It was difficult to let go of something I was so passionate about and which my world revolved around, but Dobby was my world now.'

'I've been reading about Jack Russells,' Dad went on. 'They need lots of affection.'

'And they need to get used to being on their own,' I countered.

'Don't think so,' he said.

'I don't want to argue, Dad, but I know what dogs need and don't need.'

'I have to go. You need to make important changes in your life, now you've got Dobby.'

He was right and I had made my first. Dad handed Dobby to me.

'Don't you worry, pal, Dad will never let you down,' I said holding him to my chest.

I stroked his hairy body, taking in that fresh puppy smell again and I reminded myself of where my priorities lay.

Chapter 5

A SPOONFUL OF SYRUP

I only had Dobby for a fortnight when he didn't sound right. He chewed or ate everything in the garden. He often choked if something didn't fit in his mouth. If he did swallow a bit of twig, we would know, as it arrived with his next poop. But this time, he did not choke, nor did he bark. It sounded like he was coughing. I never knew a dog to cough. I got him to open his mouth, and I wriggled my fingers inside, moving them around, checking if anything was stuck. Not finding anything, I withdrew my hand and asked Mum to check later. But when Mum inspected his mouth, she couldn't find anything.

A few days passed and he was no better. His coughs were more frequent. Every cough had me sweating, frozen to the spot. He was only three months old. Was I going to lose the wee guy so soon?

Panicking, I called the vet and explained Dobby's symptoms to the receptionist. I had heard of puppies not making it because of a hidden illness and didn't want my dog to be one of them. She placed me on hold while she spoke to the vet. They wanted to see him the same morning. I called Mum to let her know.

'Where are you, Mum?' I asked when she answered her mobile.

'I'm on my way to St Andrews, why?'

'I need you to come home.'

'Why, what is it?' she asked, speaking into her hands free phone set.

'The vet wants me to bring Dobby in for eleven.'

'Urgh, fine. Yeah, okay. I'm on my way. I'll see you in ten,' she said before ending the call.

When Mum arrived for us, she placed his crate on the ground. At the sight of it, he bolted. Mum chased him around the garden. Catching him, she gently lowered him inside. Mum carried the box to the car while I locked up. I sat in the back with Dobby. I should have done this when we brought him home, so that he was comforted and close to his dad. The back seats of cars are a struggle for me to get into. However, with some effort, I manoeuvred myself in. Dobby's crate lay on the seat beside me. My hand rested lightly on top as I looked at his confused face through the bars.

'I don't know what's happening to him, Mum,' I yelled, listening to his tongue smacking his lips. He's making little retching sounds now.'

'Hang on a minute,' Mum called back. 'There's a lay-by up here, I'll stop and have a look.'

Hurrying to locate the clips securing his door, I wrenched it open, almost detaching it from its hinges; pulled him out, and held his trembling body to my chest. Stroking his head, and assuring him that everything would be okay, I calmed him a little.

'He's been sick, Mum,' I said, feeling vomit drip onto my jacket.

'He's pooped, too,' said Mum , once she had stopped and opened the passenger-side door. 'It's on your jacket as well.'

'Don't worry about me,' I replied. 'The quicker we get him to the vet's the better.'

Mum used the wipes, rubbed sick and poop from Dobby's coat; my jacket, and cleaned the crate. Thankfully, we made it to the vet's without any more accidents. We left the crate behind, and Mum carried him in. If I ever had an excuse to take Dobby to the vet, this would be it.

Zoe is one of six friendly receptionists who work at Provost Vet Group in St Andrews, one of three practices in the area. I later learned that Zoe has had fifteen years' experience as a vet's receptionist, interacting with people and their pets. This was clear when we took Dobby for his free health check and registered him. Her friendliness and warmth stood out during his first and subsequent visits.

Dobby's breeder insisted I take out a 'vacs for life' plan through Pets at Home. This way I would only pay a one-off £100. We had a vet three miles from home but a friend of Mum's recommended Provost Vet, so I chose to register him there instead. Besides, this was a twenty-minute drive instead of forty-five minutes to our nearest Pets at Home store. The breeder's nearest store was a five-minute drive for her. I didn't want to rely on Mum and Dad going all that way every time there was something wrong with my dog. I was happy with a nearby vet and to pay for a monthly plan.

'Dobbbyyyy,' Zoe called, as we entered the vet's.

'Aye, we're back again,' I replied.

'Oh, he's so cute,' she said, coming across to fuss over him.

'Aye, only when he wants to be.'

'Is he a bit naughty?'

'Ah, he's not too bad.'

As well as Zoe, a couple more of the vet receptionists dashed from their stations to greet and cuddle him, each holding a treat. Did Dobby like this place more than me? Having a dog had unexpected benefits. With all the receptionists being female, I was going to enjoy bringing Dobby to this place. It turned my stomach to realise that I was thinking such things when Dobby was so sick. Dobby was a fluffy pup with a clean bill of health, despite his breeder lying about having a murmur in his heart. He was gorgeous. But what was this cough?

'Dobby,' a soft voice called.

'Yes, that's me, I mean him,' I said, correcting myself.

The vet gestured us through with a wave of her hand and with Mum in front, I followed behind with Dobby. We entered the consultation room, and the vet placed him on the examination table, while I sat down.

It's like us going to see the doctor. We go to see about what we have or have had. When we get there, the symptoms have disappeared, or we can't describe what we went for. But how can a dog tell you what's wrong. Apparently, dogs are good at hiding discomfort. And Dobby was no different.

'What's up with you then, wee man?' the vet asked, with a hint of American in her voice.

Did she expect Dobby or me to answer?

'It's difficult to explain,' I began. 'I know he picks up a lot of things and chokes if something doesn't fit. But this is different.'

'I see,' she replied, checking him over. 'What sort of noise does he make?'

My eyes darting around, I said, 'It's like a raspy cough.'

'He seems to be fine now,' she assured me. 'However,' she went on, 'he's most likely picked up kennel cough. It's common for a pup his age. How many siblings does he have?'

I had to think…

'He had eight brothers and sisters. Oh, wait, did he?' After some thought, I confirmed, 'Yes, he did.'

'It's likely he picked it up from them,' she said. 'It's nothing to worry about,' she went on. 'If you pick up a bottle of children's cough medicine up from the chemist.'

'Children's cough medicine?' I questioned with a furrowed brow.

'Yes,' she said. 'We give dogs many remedies designed for children.'

'How do I give it to him?' I asked.

'Your dad and I will help,' Mum interjected.

'The one you need to get will come with a syringe, so you can squirt it into his mouth.'

'Okay, that's fine,' I said. 'How long do I give him that for?'

'Two weeks and he should be fine,' she said with a satisfied smile.

The phone rang on our way out. And it was only then I learned the name of who first fussed over Dobby when we first visited Provost Vet. When she answered the phone, she introduced herself as Zoe.

Mum hadn't managed to get what she needed from St Andrews, so dropped us home first. She stopped again to wipe up more poop and sick. But this time I held him on my lap the rest of the way back. Once home, I flaked out on my stomach on the kitchen floor. I felt four tiny paws crawl up my legs and nestle in between them. I remember the day we got him home. He'd positioned himself under my kitchen chair below me, seeking security. This was different. As well as security, this was comfort and affection. We both lay for a bit until we fell asleep. I was awakened by my ringing mobile. The voiceover read out the caller display as Mum calling. I pulled the phone from my pocket and answered.

'What kind of medicine did the vet say to get?' she asked.

'I can't remember,' I said. 'One with a syringe.'

'None of these say if they come with a syringe.'

She mentioned a couple of brands that would work over the phone, and I thought I remembered. 'Yes,' I said. 'I think it was that one.'

When she got the medicine home, it didn't have a syringe, so dad picked one up. All three of us tried administering the medicine using the syringe but Dobby refused. He clenched his jaws shut. We distracted him with a toy. One of us held his bum while the other tried to wriggle a finger in between his teeth enough to poke the syringe into. But no syringe was getting into his mouth, he made sure of that. Instead, we opted for a spoon. Dobby enjoyed licking up the syrupy liquid. Thankfully. A couple of weeks later, as the vet suggested, he was better. And just as well because I wanted Dobby for a long time, not a short time. His tail swished through the air as he played in the garden again.

Chapter 6

DOBBY'S GARDENS

Dobby had two gardens. As he was a family dog, he would be brought up in two homes: Mum and Dad's, and because he was my dog, my home was his home. Both gardens were equally his to roam about in and play. They were similar in size but very different. My garden had gone through a lot of changes since I moved into my house at Dreelside in October 2006. The garden had a wheelchair ramp which almost stretched to the bottom fence.

I asked the council to take this hindrance away. I do have a wheelchair, but it would be a long time before I needed a ramp. There was life in the old legs yet.

I kept the shed although it was falling to bits, it was handy for storing the wheelchair. The rest of the garden was chipped, with one row of slabs which ran in a C-shape from my doorstep to my gate, along one side of the high fence and along the bottom fence.

Perhaps this was to aid the wheelchair user before me. Chips were not ideal for my feet, so, in 2008, I asked a gardener friend to put slabs down. I could have asked the council to slab the garden, but they would have told me to get someone else to do it. He still charged me of course and wrote me a receipt which I planned to send to the council but never did.

As well as being a hardy fisherman for many years, Dad was also a handyman, and a good bricklayer. I could have asked him to lay the slabs. I'm sure he would have done it and would have saved me a lot of money, but he had enough to do. He would only have weekends to lay slabs, and I didn't want to take his weekends away from him.

As Mum and Dad's garden was on a slope, it required lots of careful planning. Dad constructed a small wall around their garden with a lawn in the centre. A cut-out area at the bottom for sitting was created in front of the kitchen window and a raised concrete block was added at the top for the shed to sit on. A row of chips down the left-hand side completed the picture.

Dad had puppy-proofed my garden by nailing planks of wood around the bottom of each fence ages before I got Dobby. That was for the first dog I went to view.

~~~

Friends had helped source a black and tan female cocker-jack which I went to see in Musselburgh, East Lothian, but my heart was set on a male pedigree Jack Russell. I think they were trying to put me off the scent of a pure-bred Jack. However, I went to view the dog anyway.

Mum and Dad drove me to see her, but the puppy was not my ideal choice—it was a dark dog for a start. A stocky man with horn-rimmed glasses and curly brown hair met us at the door as we approached. He had a kind voice and sounded
~~~

in his forties. But something didn't feel right as he led us in.

'There she is then,' he said, opening the pen door.

I heard a small thing tumbling around happily on cushions, as Dad leant in and picked her out.

The man's jaw dropped. I didn't think he anticipated us handling her. What did he expect? Dad gently lowered her into my arms. I cuddled her close. I felt something cool and wet on my cheek. She had given me a kiss as she wriggled.

'What d'you think?' the man said.

'She's lovely,' I mumbled.

'D'you have a name for her?' he asked, folding his arms.

I had the feeling he thought the deal was done.

'Yes, Luna!'

'That's an interesting name.'

'It's a character from Harry Potter.'

'Do you want her then?'

I didn't like being pressured into anything, but I finally had a puppy in my arms, and she had a name! But you have to be sure. You shouldn't plump for the first puppy you view, especially if something doesn't feel right.

He had no paperwork, no certificates, no vet checks, no microchip. However, after agonising for what felt like hours, I decided to take her. I handed him £550, and he went to fetch a receipt—at least I was getting a receipt!

'You're not sure?' Dad said.

'No, something's odd. I want her, but he has nothing. He could be anyone. What do you think I should do?' I asked, running a thumb along Luna's back.

'If you're not sure, don't take her. There'll be other dogs,' he said.

'I can't really see her properly anyway.'

The man returned and I told him I had changed my mind.

'Oh,' he said, his arms falling to his side. 'Why?'

'I can't. Not without any paperwork, I'm sorry. She should be vaccinated and chipped.'

'But you can get that done at the vet's for a tenner.'

'That's not for me to do. It's meant to be done first.'

He stood there for a long time in silence, probably hoping I would change my mind, before explaining that he was not a breeder, and that the puppy's mother was a working dog accidently 'nicked' by a Jack Russell and that he was selling the puppies. A likely story! Perhaps it was true, but I wasn't willing to risk it. Disappointed, he handed the money back and put Luna back in her pen, leaving us to make our way out.

~~~

I was never a fan of plants so for years didn't have any in my garden. That was until a different gardener friend had insisted that I brighten things up. I gave in, bought a load of plants and let him plant them. Once grown, the garden did look more colourful. Even I could see the vibrant purple flowers on the bush flourishing in the corner. All the others had survived two harsh coastal winters.

'What's he into, now?' I asked Dad one day I heard Dobby chewing on a plant.

'He's at that… you know the one that looks like a…'

'Pull it out then,' I said. 'I can't have him eating the plants. They might get stuck in his throat.'
~~~

'Okay,' Dad said, ripping them out.

'Is there not a chive plant over here?' I asked, indicating to the side of the shed.

'Aye, I think it is,' he replied.

'They're poisonous to dogs,' I shrieked.

Plants were a waste of time, anyway. I couldn't maintain a garden and as much as I preferred Dobby not to eat them, he was doing me a favour. Dobby was into everything, and not just the plants… he picked up flowers, leaves and sticks, and even began taking my shed apart. He often appeared with a chunk of wood between his teeth, which used to belong to the shed. I think he thought he was bringing his dad a present, but the only thing he received was a telling off.

'No, Dobby, leave it,' I would say, but ignored me and kept at it.

Mum and Dad's garden was different. They had plants, too. But they were in pots and Dobby never seemed to show any interest in them. However, he investigated other areas of the garden, including his grandad's hosepipe. Mum thought it was hilarious when she discovered water gathering behind the bins. Dobby had sunk his teeth into the rubber hose and water was squirting everywhere. She didn't feel the same when she found a hole in her favourite slippers or when he kept stealing toilet rolls from the downstairs toilet. He was smart … he was devious … he would make sure no one was looking before trying his luck.

One night in early October, I was at Mum's for tea.

'Where's Dobby?' I asked, sipping on a cuppa.

'He's outside' Mum replied.

'He's very quiet.'

I didn't like Dobby being outside too much. I preferred to know where he was, keep an eye on him, and therefore didn't allow him in his own garden unattended too much. Mum and Dad's garden was different. He was often outside, but they could see what he was up to where I couldn't.

'I'll go check,' Mum said.

My heart missed a beat when Mum burst back in and started putting her shoes on.

'What is it?' I asked.

'He's gone. I'll have to find him,' she said, throwing on her coat.

My cup of tea left my stomach, travelling back up my throat, but stopped short of erupting out of my mouth. I heard the panic in her voice as Mum frantically called his name, running along the back path. I wished that, for a few minutes anyway, I had my sight back so I could help Mum look. Instead, I sat helpless, chewing my fingernails. A few minutes later, however, I heard Mum again. A little calmer now, beginning to sound annoyed.

'There you are. What are you doing in there? Get back here,' I heard her say.

Dobby had found his way into next door's garden. Although Mum and Dad's garden was enclosed, there had always been a small gap at one end of the wall where it didn't meet the house. I knew this because I used to squeeze through the gap for a shortcut to next door when I was young. Dobby had done the same. I also remembered there was a hole in the fence at the far side of the neighbour's garden so he could have gone through that too, but he didn't. I knew from that day Dobby would never run far from us because, although he was only a few weeks old, he was loyal to his family.

Chapter 7

TRAINING AND TREATS

Dobby had been raised in a cage, so the breeder provided one as part of the purchase. Dad built this as soon as we got back but ideally it should be assembled prior to bringing a puppy home. We didn't know. He was toilet trained before we collected him, but I was sceptical. Was this possible? He was eleven weeks old and the length of my forearm. The breeder let him, along with his eight siblings, outside to do the toilet and she assured me this worked.

I'd hoped the breeder was right and it might not happen, but I constantly felt something wet and warm seep through my sock. It smelled sweet but stale as I crawled around the floor sniffing for it. I grabbed some kitchen roll and lowered myself to my knees. After a few minutes sniffing and feeling around, I found it and mopped it up. Toilet-trained my arse; I muttered as I deposited kitchen roll in the bin.

It was warm enough to leave the back door open so Dobby could run in and out. Apparently, you shouldn't do this. You train a dog to go out to do his business then come back in. That way you know what he's done or not done. Dobby preferred to come in from outside to pee instead of the other way around. I found another, and another. I stepped in it, knelt in it and put my hands in it. I wasn't finding poop in the house since the first night… thankfully; he did that in the garden, preferring the chips to the slabs.

Rearing a puppy with my poor eyesight was proving a challenge. Resigned to needing help, I phoned *See Scape*, my local blind society. Although they don't have much to do with dogs, I knew they had clients with guide dogs.

~~~

In 2004 I had considered a guide dog, so arranged for an assessment. I thought a dog would help me get around, but I was kidding myself. How was I going to cope with poor mobility and two crutches, especially as I wouldn't be able to use them in the assessment? However, the prospect of owning a dog excited me. In preparation, I tried to get fitter and stronger by using a metal walking stick. I sensed from the moment I opened the door to the assessor I wasn't going to pass. She fulfilled her duty and went through the process, acting as the dog. I held a makeshift harness in one hand and the walking stick in the other. It was hopeless. I tripped and stumbled, almost falling on the woman. I tried to convince her I would build myself up by going to the gym. Who was I kidding? I was unfit to have a guide dog. If I was unsuitable for a dog then, why was this different with Dobby? Both my mobility and eyesight have deteriorated since then.

~~~

I phoned my local Blind Society, explaining about Dobby and asking for help. My key worker called back later with advice.

'Hi, Billy, it's Evelyn.'

'Thanks for getting back to me,' I said.

'You've been getting a puppy,' she said.

'That's right. He's a great wee thing, but he can do with training.'

'What kind of dog is he?'

'A Jack Russell terrier.'

'Ah, one of those. They're great family dogs.'

'Aye they are.'

'Sorry I've taken a while,' she continued. 'I wanted to make sure I had something for you.'

'That's okay,' I said, expecting good news.

'My colleague has a puppy and used dog training classes in Anstruther.'

I knew who she was referring to. She was also vision impaired. If she could do it, so could I.

'That's handy,' I said, interrupting.

'Yes, she said the trainer was great.'

Evelyn knew the name of the classes but had nothing specific. It wasn't the advice I hoped for, but I thanked her for her help.

~~~

I double-tapped my iPhone screen to open Facebook. Using the voiceover function, I swiped across the screen until I reached the menu. A slow process but it allows blind and partially sighted people to operate smart phones. Locating
~~~

the search box, I entered *Coastal Paws Dog Training*. A list of matches appeared, and I scrolled down until I found the right one. The training was held by a local woman I had heard of but had never met. I brought up her contact details and called the number, but it went to voicemail. I left a message. A few days passed and I'd heard nothing, so I went back onto Facebook and found a different number. The same happened, but I didn't leave a message. Would I have to train Dobby on my own?

I stood in the garden checking what Dobby was up to. The sunlight was hampering my vision when my phone rang. Turning away from the sun, I pulled the phone from my pocket. Voiceover read out a number I didn't recognise, but I took the call.

'Hi, is this Billy?' a voice asked.

'Who's this?'

'Fiona from Coastal Paws.'

'Yes, yes, it's me.'

'So, you want to enrol your dog for training,' she said.

'Aye, I do. I mean, he's a good dog but he's into everything,'

'What sort of thing would you like from your dog?'

'To leave things when I tell him and come when he's called.'

'Don't you have bad eyesight?' she asked, a doubt in her voice.

'Yes, I do, is that a problem?' I asked, fearing the worst. Was she going to turn me away like the guide-dog woman?

'Not at all,' she asserted. 'I'd like to visit you at home, if that's ok?'

'Absolutely.'

We agreed on a date and time. Meanwhile, I placed puppy training mats on the kitchen floor—ones with adhesive corners. Sometimes this worked. Sometimes it didn't. After patting my hand across the mat and finding a warm puddle, I praised him. If I found a warm patch on the floor, I told him off, ushering him to the door. Training mats give off a scent to encourage the dog to use them. The trouble was, Dobby would rather clamp his teeth on a corner of a mat and drag it outside to rip to shreds. Sometimes I caught him and sometimes I didn't. I changed tactics. Restricting him to the kitchen was still difficult, so I allowed him into the living room, placing a pad in front of the settee. With somewhere else to try, I thought it might work. It didn't. The only advantage was he had further to travel with the mat trailing along the ground, making it easier to catch him. I abandoned the training pads and tried the old-fashioned way. If he began circling and sniffing, it was a sign he needed out. As soon as I was aware of this, I called his name, pointed to the door and chased him out. I wanted to have something mastered before Fiona came.

I asked Mum to be present and when Fiona arrived, she let her in, ushering her into the living room where I sat waiting.

'This must be Dobby.' She stroked him as he pawed her leg.

'Aye, it is,' I said.

I stayed where I was. Mum perched on the arm of the couch beside me, while Fiona plonked herself on the end of the settee, placing her bag on the floor. I visualised her with short and spikey hair like she had put her finger in an electric socket. After she left, however, Mum told me her hair was swept back into a ponytail. Over the phone, she sounded gruff and stubborn, a stern young woman, possibly early thirties, a force to be reckoned with, whereas Fiona was relaxed in her seat with crossed legs and wearing a broad, dazzling smile.

'So, from what you've told me, Dobby's a mischievous wee thing,' she said, folding her arms across her chest, reminding me of the woman on the phone.

'He can be.'

'Okay, we'll get that sorted.' She reached into her handbag.

Dobby was curious to know what was in her bag; he already had his snout in it. She had the magical gift. When she told him no, he stopped. Fiona pulled two items out and placed them beside her, but Dobby's nose was back in her bag. She reached in for something else. It was like a can of deodorant. She pressed the trigger, and he backed away.

'You won't like that, Dobby!'

The first thing she asked was if I had puppy training mats.

'Yes, but I gave up on them. He was dragging them outside.'

Mum brought her one and she laid it at her feet.

'Gradually move them towards the back door. An inch or two at a time. He'll learn the closer the mat gets to the door is the route to pee.'

'But he keeps dragging them outside,' I said raising my eyebrows.

'The more you persist, the more he'll learn.'

Now that was out the way, she moved on to getting him to let items go.

'How d'you want to do this?'

'Depends on what I've to do.'

'A bit of tuggy and reward.'

'I'm better kneeling,' I said, lowering myself to the floor.

She placed a rope toy between Dobby and me, instructing me to hold out my hand.

'What's that?' Mum asked.

'Smoked sausage.' She tipped some into my hand. 'Dogs love them. Cut them into small pieces and keep them in the fridge.'

One of my rules had been broken. I was clear from the start; Dobby was not getting human food. But who was I to argue with a dog trainer!

'Okay, put your hand on the rope,' she said.

I did as she told me.

'Now drag it towards you, let him take it and tell him a command to leave it.'

I did this, too.

'He'll want to keep hold of the rope but if he lets go, let him have it back,' she went on. 'If he lets go, give him a treat, and praise him. If he doesn't let go, offer the treat but don't give it immediately. Repeat this until he knows the reward is for doing something right.'

She showed us other tasks. For example, she told Mum to take him into the kitchen, asked me to tell him a wait command, hold my treat hand out, and tell him to come. This worked. Despite earlier reservations, her training session helped. I had renewed confidence.

'Anything else?' she asked.

'What about him sniffing on walks?' I asked.

'Cut that out. Keep him close at all times and when he

sniffs give the lead a wee tug and say leave it. Always keep his focus on you.'

'How much does Billy owe you?' Mum asked when we finished.

'Nothing, as long as you attend my classes,' she insisted.

'When are they?' I asked.

'The next block starts in early November,' she said, packing her bag.

'Okay, we'll be there,' I assured her.

While Mum and Fiona talked, I was listening to what Dobby was up to.

'Oy,' I yelled.

Mum and Fiona jumped.

'What is it?' Mum asked.

'He's doing something behind the couch,'

'That command worked,' Fiona said. 'Use it. Jack Russells are very intelligent.'

'Yeah, too intelligent,' I agreed.

'He listened though. His head popped up.'

As Mum showed her out, I heard Fiona say, 'He's a good dog, I've dealt with worse at his age.'

I sat back on the couch with a satisfied sigh.

Chapter 8

THE HISTORY OF THE JACK RUSSELL

There are so many varieties of dog, it is hard to believe they all descended from the same ancestor, the grey wolf. Although scientists find it hard to say when dogs became domesticated by humans, most current theories based on genetic studies indicate the origins were in the Middle East between 12,000 and 20,000 years ago. Generations of selective breeding, coupled with the current trend for designer dogs, has seen the number of different types increase, making classification for the International Kennel Clubs and breed registration clubs around the world problematic.

In the past dogs were categorised according to their skills and subsequently what they did or what they could be used for. These tended to be working dogs used in farming and hunting. At this time, they were not grouped by appearance. Although we still have dogs for rounding up sheep or cattle or for hunting, and many are now employed in the police or armed services, most of the estimated 12.5 million in the UK are pets. Nowadays, however, selective breeding for every set of characteristics has created a plethora of different crossbreeds. Dogs are bred for size, shape and colour or hair length and since the end of the last century the number of different types has risen steadily. However, not many are recognised by the Kennel Club as distinctive breeds.

The situation is similar with Jack Russell terriers. Even the different names given to this type of dog can cause confusion. However, what is known is the origin of the dog and the development of the breed is well documented. In the early nineteenth century John Russell, better known as Jack, enjoyed hunting with dogs during his school days in Devon. While studying to become a clergyman at the University of Oxford, Jack met a milkman with a fox terrier. He recognised that this bitch, called Trump, had the boldness, tenacity and colouring needed to make a perfect hunting dog. Trump had a dense, white wire coat with dark tan patches over her eyes, ears and the base of her tail. Jack persuaded the milkman to sell her, and Trump became the founding bitch for Russell's new line of hunting dogs.

When Russell returned to Devon in 1832, as parson of Swimbridge, he continued to work on fine-tuning this line, improving their stamina, wits and colouring. White dogs were easier to see in the fields and were less likely to be mistakenly shot by hunters. He also bred them so the dogs could make decisions without human direction, finding short-cuts in land where they had never hunted before and barking to alert hunters to where the quarry was. The word terrier derives from 'terre' meaning ground or earth. The Reverend Russell's dogs were bred to 'go to earth' in search of quarry such as foxes or badgers. They were expected to be fearless and determined but not aggressive and without bloodlust, prepared to face up to larger opponents. They were not intended to be killers although they proved to be good for vermin control.

In 1873, the Reverend Russell helped fund the Kennel Club, the world's first registry for all canine breeds. Although he judged competitions, he never showed as he felt his dogs were for working and wanted to maintain a clear distinction. Jack Russell died in 1883 but in 1894, the first Parson Jack Russell Club was established to continue the breeding programme he had begun, sourcing as many of Trump's descendants as possible. Over time the Parson Russell terrier standard established by the Reverend Russell has been bred with many other dogs and there is no consistency amongst breeders. Despite this, breed stalwarts have attempted to maintain the dog developed by Parson Jack and the breed was officially recognised by the Kennel Club as recently as 1990. In 1999, the name was changed to Parson Russell terrier which is now the official name of the Kennel Club registered breed. However, the Jack Russell still doesn't have an official registration. This confusion over naming can be simplified as follows:

- The Parson Russell terrier is a bigger dog standing around twelve to fifteen inches and is registered with the Kennel Club meaning it can be exhibited in the show ring.
- The Jack Russell terrier looks broadly similar to the Parson but is built for work and is not eligible for Kennel Club competition.
- The Pet Jack Russell has shorter legs, standing

around ten to twelve inches, and is a favourite
with dog lovers, making a great family pet.

The vast majority are now pets but since they all come from the same source, the terrier side of their character is never far from the surface.

All three types are built for speeds of up to thirty miles per hour but also for endurance and can run for hours without tiring. This is true of Dobby. When he chases a ball, the sound reminds me of a tiny horse's hooves thudding through the grass. On the other hand, once he is home, he curls up but is never fully asleep. He tends to keep one eye open in case something happens to catch his attention. This is evident when he hears the slightest noise such as a vehicle pulling up, a car door slamming or even Granny or Grandad's footsteps approaching the back gate. He is then instantly alert and often runs to the back door assuming it's for him.

When it comes to coat, colouring and markings, Russell terriers have mainly the same physical characteristics. They have a double coat which has a coarse texture and should be hairy or wiry and dense, but never woolly as woolliness retains wetness. The type of coat varies from smooth to rough. While a smooth coat allows a comb to move through effortlessly, making for easy grooming, a rough coat will require a bit more exertion when combing. The most usual type is something in between. This is referred to as a broken coat and is accompanied by eyebrows and a beard.

A Russell terrier's coat is an important part of their armoury, protecting them from the undergrowth and the teeth and claws of the animals they were developed to hunt. The thick coat also protects against all weathers, keeping them warm and dry in wind and rain, or even freezing temperatures. As a result, I have been reluctant to put any sort of protective jacket on Dobby as he already has a natural one. The Russell terrier's colouring is at least fifty percent white with tan, brown or black markings on the head, ears, back and tail. There is no standard to how these markings are arranged, and they tend to be unique to each dog, and can even be a mixture of all three colours.

It is thanks to the Reverend Jack Russell that I found my perfect companion. The first time I set eyes on a Jack Russell was in 1997. A friend had brought her dog, called Marley, along when we hung out. He was pure white—or that's what I thought. Even then, my eyesight was poor, he looked white, but he wasn't. She told me his markings were faint and he had black ears. I remember him sitting beside me on a small wall. He was one of the best behaved, and most beautiful dogs I had ever seen. I told myself that if I ever got a dog, I wanted one exactly like him.

Sourcing Marley's double was nigh on impossible. Dobby's breeder had two males left and after I explained my circumstances, she believed that the bigger of the two would be better for me. He was the whiter of the two, on his front half anyway. As I couldn't see what he looked like in any pictures, I trusted the judgement of others. It was difficult to distinguish which type of Russell Dobby was.

His muzzle and face are white, but his ears are tan. A white stripe, about one-inch-wide stretches over his head, spreading out like a river reaching the sea as it moves along his spine to his tail. He has tan markings on his back which resemble an angel's wings. He also has tan patches around his eyes and the first part of his tail. The top of his legs is tan, but he has black speckles on his belly. His claws are white but his front right and hind left paws each have a single black claw. Oh, and he has white eyebrows and a white beard.

This makes him distinctly a Jack Russell terrier which makes sense since his mother was a Kennel Club registered Parson, but his father was a Pet Jack Russell. Despite a lot of brown, he normally appears white to me—especially when he is motionless against my dark flooring. On the other hand, when he lies on my white bed covers, he looks brown and when he runs, I see a brown flash dart past. Despite Jack Russells being bred to hunt, Dobby is not fearless. He's caught a few mice but flinches at the slightest movement of a bush or leaf and he has a tremble in his bark when something spooks him.

Chapter 9

EYE ON THE PRIZE

Dobby loves playing with his dad chasing yellow tennis balls. I lie on my front in the living room and throw the ball into the kitchen. Dobby runs after it and brings it back. Sometimes I throw it behind me, so he has to clamber over me to retrieve it. Once he's had enough, he crawls onto my back, lies down and begins licking my ear.

Another of Dobby's favourite games is tug of war—tuggy. I remember wrestling with my friend's Jack Russell, Zack, using an old tea towel. I swung him from side to side. But Zack was two. Dobby was only twelve weeks, but I wanted him to learn when he was a puppy. Jean Donaldson, in her book *The Culture Clash*, says, '…tug of war is a tremendous predatory energy burner and good exercise for both dog and owner.'

I found a tea towel and presented it to him. Waving it from side to side, I watched him track it before letting him take hold. Unfortunately, after our initial game every tea towel looked like a tuggy toy to Dobby.

'What's that towel doing on the floor?' Dad asked one night.

'It's okay, it's an old one. I was playing tuggy with Dobby.'

'What did you do that for?'

'We were playing.'

'That was stupid. He'll think every towel is a toy.'

Dad was right again. But how did Dad know so much about dogs and what you should and shouldn't do with them? As far as I'm aware, he's never had one. Since getting Dobby, Dad had talked to a few of his customers who have dogs and was dishing advice from what they'd told him. But Dobby was my dog, and I wanted to play the way I wanted with him.

~~~

It was easier if I had things at hand, especially at the sink. My tea towel hung from a drawer. Dobby worked out that if he stood on his hind legs, he could get the towel between his teeth and whip it away. When I reached for the towel, it was gone. It was possibly on the floor, or more likely to be outside. When I retrieved it, the label was chewed off. Dobby had a fascination for labels. Everything that had once had a label, shortly didn't. Every towel—no label. The blanket over his cage—no label. My Celtic blanket—no label. If Dobby found the corner of something, this was bitten off, too. I tucked my tea towel out of reach, but he would see the slightest bit of cloth sticking out and manage to pinch it.

If something didn't look like it should be in the house, he ran outside with it. I was watching telly one night and the channels began changing. Feeling for the remote, it wasn't there.

'Dobby,' I roared, heading outside.
~~~

The channels were changing from the garden. I took it from him and returned it to its rightful place. But everything went missing. At least I knew where to find things.

~~~

Thanks to the Reverend Russell, Jacks are intelligent dogs, and Dobby is no different. He sniffs out anything, solves problems and never forgets. If he wants something, he gets it. I remember when he was five months old. A footstool sat in the middle of the living room. Positioning himself in the kitchen, Dobby ran through at top speed before sliding on his belly and crashing into the pouffe, but it only moved an inch. We thought this was hilarious. He repeated the act. Again, and again. An inch and another inch. We were bent double laughing.

But it wasn't a game… Dobby had a plan. Some DVDs, which hadn't been put away, lay on the television unit. He had already attempted to get them by putting his front paws on the edge, but he couldn't reach. He was using the pouffe as leverage. He tried to edge it close enough to snatch a DVD, run away and demolish the box. He learned he didn't have to run from the kitchen but could edge it forward using his body. He then climbed onto the pouffe, taking whatever was on the unit. All DVDs had to be put away. In fact, everything that was in easy reach had to go.

~~~

I remember cleaning piss from the living room floor with kitchen roll, then placing the roll on the couch. I forgot about it. He couldn't climb onto the couch, or could he? Later, I went to get the kitchen roll. The garden! I was too late. The roll was scattered everywhere. If he wanted to clean up his own piss, he was welcome. Saved me from doing it. Later, I found two DVD boxes on the living room floor—one of which had the cover ripped off. If he wanted a choice of movie, he could have asked. Ironically, the coverless box was *Pet Sematary*.

Dad had puppy-proofed the garden, but we didn't consider the living room. The coffee table was cluttered with letters, CDs, photographs—memorabilia which were important to me. A picture of my granny and one of my niece and nephew—photos I would never get back. I managed to salvage them though. All cushions had to go. Everything was now Dobby-proofed. But he was growing fast.

When Dobby jumped onto the couch, I didn't stop him. He liked to play with his dad. I loved nothing better than roughing him around, and he enjoyed it, too. But I couldn't put up with the biting. He liked my fingers, and no matter how many times I told him off, he still bit. I sent him to his cage. I slapped his snout, not hard, but enough to tell him off. When it got too much, I asked Dad to come up.

'A customer told me, if he's biting, he thinks he's playing,' he said.

'Fair enough, but I'm not wanting him biting me.'

'They said, turn your back and face away and he'll get the message.'

I tried this, and after some time, he calmed down. Months later I learned that I should let him do it because he was testing his bite threshold. The advice was right. Dobby was judging how much pressure to apply without harming me. If he bit too hard, I said, 'OUCH,' and he stopped.

~~~

One day while playing with Dobby on the couch he had his eye on a prize. I offered him my hands, but he wasn't interested. No, it was something else. He was crawling over me, and I sensed he was looking elsewhere. The next thing I knew, I screamed as much as my lungs allowed. I think Dobby got the bigger fright. My earring was lying on the couch, my lobe bleeding profusely.

'Look what you've done to Dad! Bad boy!' I wailed as I rushed for kitchen roll.

His head hung, and his little ears dropped.

'It's okay, Dobby,' I said, petting him. 'It was an accident.'

Perhaps I should have been harder on him, but he was a quick learner. I knew he wouldn't try it again. Having cleaned my ear, I picked up the earring. It was bent and the pin was out. Luckily, he ripped it out without tearing my lobe. Despite the bloody mess, I couldn't resist picking him up and cuddling him. Mum got a new ring a few days later. Dobby has never tried to destroy his dad's ear again. He chooses to run his wet tongue around the silver, shiny loop, instead.
~~~

Chapter 10

SHOWER TIME

When we collected Dobby from Blackburn, West Lothian, the trip home was traumatic for him—an hour-and-a-half drive to Anstruther. The breeder had fed him before we picked him up, not a clever idea before a long car journey.

'Ahh, Wullie, he's been sick,' said Mum from the back seat.

Dad pulled their white Mitsubishi four-wheel drive into a layby and hurried around to the back of the car.

Leaving the passenger side, I felt my way along to join Dad at the open boot. Dad spent thirty years at sea, skippering fishing boats, but thirty years at sea does not reflect the man Dad really is. In his early sixties, with speckled grey hair, Dad stroked his well-groomed moustache as he peered through his glasses at the tiny terrier. You could describe Dad as a small terrier, but he is a gentle man who always helps anyone in need.

'How is he?' I asked, as the warm sun shone on Dobby's little face, which I was able to see close up.

'He's been sick,' Dad responded.

'Aw, Dobby,' I said, stroking his head. 'Have you anything

to clean it up with?' I added, seeing his brown eyes look up at me.

'Pass them wipes, Joanna,' he said.

'Will he be okay?' I asked.

I'd never had a dog before and thought that putting him in a carrier was the natural thing to do. His little box lay on the folded down seat next to Mum, but he should have travelled home on my lap. But we weren't to know. A connection would have formed between us if I held him on my lap.

'He's a bit shaken up,' Dad said. 'The quicker we get him home the better.'

Dad reached inside the dog carrier and gently pulled Dobby out. Using the baby wipes, he cleaned Dobby's fur before offering him some water. But he wouldn't touch any. We stopped twice more before we got him home.

Dobby does not like water. Perhaps it's no surprise. Dad washed Dobby in the sink as soon as we got to my house, removing any remaining sick before gently placing him on the kitchen floor. Dobby stood quivering. I planned to wash him in the shower but was he going to cope?

Dad gave him his first shower while I watched. I prefer the water steaming hot, but Dobby would be scalded at my setting.

'You'll can't use your temperature,' he said, turning the dial before resting the shower head on the floor.

'I know that Dad,' I said, rolling my eyes.

'And not on full power, either.'

'I know that, too.'

Dobby reminded me of Greyfriars Bobby on George IV

Bridge in Edinburgh, standing like a statue, as Dad soaked him with lukewarm water. Picking up his shampoo, Dad said, 'Take two handfuls and lather it over his body, but not his face.'

'Why not?' I asked.

'You don't want it in his eyes.'

'Dad, dog shampoo is like Johnson Baby. It's designed to go in their eyes and not sting,' I said through gritted teeth.

'Make sure you rinse it all off.'

'Aye, okay,' I said.

Dobby had chewed a corner off one of my bath towels, so I used that to dry him as much as possible. Once free, Dobby charged around the house twisting and turning, sliding on his back. Rubbing his body along the carpet; along the walls, along the furniture, in his bed—anything he could use to rub off the scent. It was a hilarious sight. The sound of the carry-on made me laugh.

It was different when I tried washing him. When he saw me approach in my boxers he seemed to know and walked away from me. I tried to follow the sound of his nails tap the floor. As I thought I'd found him, he dashed past my legs back into the living room. I chased him back into the kitchen.

'Got ya, pal,' I said, cornering him at the back door.

I gathered him under my arm and carried him through. Fortunately, I have a wet floor shower room which has a toilet, wash hand basin and shower, making it easier for me, but the distance from the kitchen is quite a long way to carry a dog, even if he was only a puppy. Once there, I placed him on the floor, adjusted the temperature then started the water, but when I laid the shower head on the floor it was upside down and the pressure was too high, so the water sprayed up like a fountain, soaking both of us—just as well I only had boxers on.

I reduced the pressure to a gentler flow. Now I was ready for him, only I couldn't find him. The door was shut so he was there somewhere. With the water still running, I crawled on my hands and knees and searched. I found him squeezed between the toilet and the wall. Picking him up again, I crawled to the shower. When I finally got water on him, he stood like a statue again. It was easy enough following Dad's instructions, but I struggled to apply enough shampoo. When I asked him to lift a paw, he did. When I asked him to lift another, he did. He was so patient allowing his dad to run his hands through his coat. Once dried, I opened the door. While Dobby ran around the house rubbing off the scent of shampoo, I melted in a soaking wet bathroom, holding an empty towel. I welled up, unable to prevent the grin forming on my face.

I look forward to this ritual every eight weeks, or if he needs washing sooner—especially if he rolls in fox poo. That is always a messy affair. Catching him has become harder. As he has got older, he has become wiser, and quicker. He jumps from couch to couch. He sneaks into my bedroom. When I go near him, he jumps on the bed. When I try to pick him up, he jumps down again. It is never, 'Dobby, shower,' and he comes. It is always a game to him.

Eventually, however, he stops leaping around and lies still. This is my cue to pick him up although he never goes willingly. He still doesn't like it, but he puts up with it. I am bent over double, clutching my sides, seeing him pelt around the house after his shower. And he does it every time. I am concerned I am upsetting him, but after his exertions around the house he snuggles up beside me on the couch. Although he's still a little bit wet he dries quickly and smells amazing, and I know he still loves me.

Chapter 11

BITTER TASTE

When I found out audio description was available in cinemas in Dundee, I wanted to go as much as I could—and at every opportunity I did—whether it be on my own, Mum and Dad dropping me off, or with volunteers. Before I got Dobby, I had a volunteer called Graham, who offered to take me when he was available, which was roughly once every two months. It was at least a seven-hour round trip for him, depending on the length of the film. This meant I couldn't go as often as I wished.

Another volunteer became available. He lived in Anstruther. He took me on Wednesdays to a blind group thirteen miles away. This was the only time Dobby was regularly left alone. I made sure he was settled before I left each week. This wasn't easy as he knew I was going out and was reluctant to go in his cage. An hour after I left, Mum let him out and took him for a walk. But I preferred Dobby to be in his cage when I returned home. He was so excited I could hear the cage rattling before I got the key in the lock. And when he saw me enter, I thought the cage would collapse, as he was so desperate to get to me.

'Hang on,' I said, lowering myself to my knees.

Like a lion pouncing on its prey, he burst from his cage as soon as the door was open. He began licking my face. I didn't mind leaving Dobby at home for a while because I knew he would be fine and the more I did this the more he realised I would come home. I always felt guilty, and I rarely left him for long periods. Things changed when my new volunteer offered to take me to the cinema.

The Odeon in Dundee was my preferred cinema. I had visited a few times on my own and was familiar with the lay-out. I got to know the names of the staff members and built a rapport with them. They said to phone directly to let them know I was coming, and they would have my headset ready and one of them would meet me. I remember one visit when a staff member saw me cross the car park and was already waiting for me. If Mum and Dad were going to Dundee, I asked them to drop me off. I went as much as possible.

However, my first trip with my new volunteer was not to the Odeon but to Cineworld. In fact, he never took me to the Odeon. He would look for films he wanted to see and let me know what showings suited. Mid-morning was better for him. I was fine with that. After all, he didn't have to take me. It meant he got in free, although he never asked for petrol money. Unfortunately, he was never reliable enough.

Going in the morning meant organising Mum to let Dobby out. I picked up sweets and juice the previous night and made sure I was up early to see to Dobby before getting ready. It was Friday 11th October, and we were due to see *IT: Chapter 2*. I was taking a shower when I heard my message tone. He phoned about ten minutes later.

'Hi Billy, did you get my message?'

'No, I'm just out of the shower.'

'Erm, something's come up and I can't make it this morning,' he said, with heavy breaths.

His excuses were probably genuine, but it became a habit. I had a dog to let out of his cage. I would have to call the Odeon and let them know I couldn't make it. And I had to let Mum know I wasn't going. Did he realise how much effort I went through just for him to take me then to cancel? It always happened when I arranged to go to the Odeon.

'Right,' I managed to say, through gritted teeth, keeping my voice level. 'Thanks for letting me know.'

I hung up and dropped my phone onto the bed, rather than throw it across the room. If I did that, I'd either have to ask someone to find it for me or get down on my hands and knees to search for it again. I could do without the hassle, or indeed, the cinema.

Despite the cancellations, I enjoyed the movies he *did* take me to see.

~~~

In 2017, after watching *IT: Chapter 1,* Graham, my original volunteer promised to take me to see *IT: Chapter 2* as soon as it was released. I remember being disappointed to learn I would have to wait two years, but I wasn't disappointed when Graham kept his promise. The showing was on Friday 18th October at the Odeon. I phoned ahead to let them know I was coming. Mum said she would take Dobby for a couple
~~~

of hours and put him in his cage for me getting home. I explained that I wouldn't be long. The cinema's dispensed Coke is overpriced so I took my own bottle but bought a bag of Pick 'n' Mix when I got there. Because I was so used to the place, I was showing Graham around, instead of him guiding me. But he helped me to my seat as it was dark, and my eyes struggled to adjust. Once he sat me down, I made myself comfortable.

The audio description was playing in my ears, but I wasn't listening; it was just distorted sounds. I didn't feel the rumble of the surround sound, just Dobby whimper when I closed his cage door. The familiar sweet aroma of popcorn was replaced by the smell of Dobby's fur. The pick 'n' mix tasted bitter, just like when I accidently swallowed a bit of his wet food.

Suddenly, I didn't want to be there. As the movie went on, I was conscious of time. I struggled to follow the film, even though I read the book beforehand and knew the plot. The movie was longer than I expected. The film was two hours in, and I did not realise there were still fifty minutes remaining. Dobby was alone and I wanted home.

It was like in Philip Pullman's *His Dark Materials* novels when each character has a daemon, an external physical manifestation of a person's 'inner self' that takes the form of an animal. When anyone is too far from, or cut off from their daemon, it hurts. And hurts badly.

It felt the same being away from Dobby. He was part of me now. I felt empty as Graham drove me home. But like that lion pouncing on its prey, he was over the moon to see his dad come home. I hurried to his cage and released him.

As soon as the door opened, he began licking my face and I didn't think he would stop. I hugged him close and breathed in his soft, hairy scent.

Chapter 12

THE ERSKINE HALL

It was the 30th of October when Dad drew up outside the Erskine Hall, a few minutes before six, where Fiona instructed the Good Citizen Dog Scheme. I liked to feed Dobby, and Dad to walk him before leaving the house. We would attend her classes each Wednesday for the next eight weeks. Dobby would receive a foundation certificate at the end of it. We heard the barking bursting from the building before Dad stopped the car. I hadn't set foot in the place for almost twenty years. How much sight had I lost since then? Would this be harder for Dobby, or for me?

The Erskine Hall was originally a church, built between 1850 and 1852. In the 1900s, the church changed its purpose, becoming a centre for the unemployed and later a Sunday School. It had many functions before it was taken over by the council in 1980. The Erskine Hall has a large hall with a kitchen, toilets and full disabled access. I used to attend a youth club twice a week in the late nineties. The club had been based in the East Neuk Centre but moved to the Erskine Hall.

Dad, Dobby and I waited in the confined vestibule while the other class finished. My heart was pounding against my rib cage. But I had a dog to train. We spoke to other owners, while Dobby was busy pulling on the retractable lead attached to my belt, trying to speak to other dogs.

My reaction to the hall was as I had feared. It made me realise just how much my vision had deteriorated since my teens.

'Where d'you want to sit?' Dad asked, entering the hall.

'I don't know, I've not been here for years,' I said, Dobby pulling one way, Dad guiding me the other.

Dad settled me in a seat half-way down the right-hand-side in front of the large radiator, which I remembered. Did the seat have to be red? Red is a colour I find difficult to distinguish. At least the floor was blue. If the floor had been green, I would've been snookered. The floor had been wood coloured before, bumpy and uneven, but it had been refurbished and levelled.

'How many dogs are here, Dad?' I whispered, under the sound of barking.

A friend who took his dog to the same classes warned me it would be noisy, and unbearable at times.

'Thirteen,' Dad answered.

'Thirteen.' I scanned the room with what sight I had, picking out shapes dotted around the room.

'Aye, there's an Irish setter, a dachshund, a big fluffy thing which looks like the dog from the Andrex advert and a few collies,' he said.

Dad mentioned a few breeds, but there were many more I couldn't remember. I tried to pick them out as Fiona made her way to the bottom of the hall and stepped onto the stage.

If I remembered correctly, there had been a stage before, which had a pool table and piano. This was where the girls from youth club assembled, but I can't remember what they got up to.

The East Neuk Centre was different. It was bigger. It was better. There was more to do. It had a larger hall where the boys spent most of their time—playing football, hockey, basketball, among other things. It had a communal area with a pool table, a lounge area with a telly in the corner and a tuck shop. It also had a back office, where the girls sometimes disappeared to, and I often joined them. We shared stories, played games and sang along to songs on the ghetto blaster. I remember singing along to *Rotterdam or Anywhere,* and *Don't Marry Her,* both by the Beautiful South in 1996 and being shocked on hearing one of the girls substituting swear words into the lyrics of the latter. I was unaware of the explicit version. I tried to impress this particular girl with Chumbawamba's song, *Tub Thumping,* by singing the lyric 'Danny Boy' at such a high pitch. I can still remember Amanda's lop-sided smile, with tears running down her cheeks as she tipped her head to one side, holding her stomach. The strands of her long blonde hair came loose from her ponytail as her head bobbed around. She usually wore a light blue top with tight white trousers. A row of gleaming white teeth always sparkled at you, along with her piercing blue eyes.

The vision faded when Fiona cleared her throat, and I was back in the room.

'Okay,' she began, regaining my attention. 'Your dog will have accidents; they are still developing. If your dog happens to mess, there is a mop and bucket in the corner here.' She indicated it with her hand.

Fiona waved her arms like she was using a baton to direct an ensemble of musicians.

'Right,' she continued. 'It is the law that your dog should be microchipped. This should have been done by a vet before you brought your dog home. I also encourage you to take out an insurance plan and health cover. If you haven't done this, please do so before next week's class.'

A warmth radiated through my body; the corners of my mouth rose. I'd done something right.

One of the first exercises was to walk in a circle around the hall with our dog. Simple as it seemed, it was far from it. I had Dobby's retractable lead attached to my belt and began walking around the hall with everyone else, Dad by my side. As expected, the rest of the dogs, and their owners walked a lot quicker than me. I heard Fiona's voice say, 'It is important to prevent your dog from sniffing. If you don't, then it will be difficult to stop your dog while out on walks. Keep your dog by your side and tell him off if he pulls to the side. Give him a reward if he stops.'

I felt Dad's hand fumble my side.

'What are you doing?' I asked.

'I need the lead,' he answered.

'No, I need it,' I countered, keeping a tight hold of my belt. 'He's my dog,' I went on. 'I need to be able to train him.'

Not satisfied, he tried to whip the lead from me, but because it was attached, he fumbled for the eyelet and unbuck-led my belt. He could have released the catch from Dobby's collar, but he wanted control. Dad left me rooted to the spot. I had lost my bearings from being asked to walk in a circle. I felt like a plonker, everyone passing me several times.

When Fiona called a halt on the exercise, Dad returned and guided me to my seat.

'That thing's not doing any good,' Dad expressed, whipping Dobby's harness off.

I sat in stony silence, not wanting to answer him.

Another task was to teach the dogs to be attentive to their name. I rose from my seat when Fiona asked all dog owners to stand at a short distance from their dog. I no longer had my lead, so Dad told me to sit down and watch. How was I supposed to watch when I couldn't see? It seemed like an easy task. All that the owner had to do was stand a short distance away and call the dog's name. All that the dog had to do was look at you, even if it was for just a few seconds. Dobby was successful because he responded to his name. But he was responding to Dad's voice, and not mine.

'I could have managed that, Dad!' I said, when he sat down.

'I think it's best if I do the training and you take it in. I'll let you know what you have to do later.'

'Whatever, Dad,' I moaned, scanning the room for nothing in particular.

I anticipated the next few weeks would be frustrating. What was the point in going to training and not actually training my dog? I wasn't letting Dad carry out *all* the training, because I knew he wouldn't explain everything to me later.

There were tasks I could actually take part in. Letting Dobby play with other dogs and interact with their owners; being able to handle him, and check his health and well-being were manageable. The last task of the night was a challenge, and a challenge I had to perform myself—one of the reasons I had enrolled my dog for training.

'Now,' Fiona began. We are going to see how far along your dog is by doing a bit of re-call. When I call your dog's name, I'll ask you to walk your dog to me. I will then ask you to make your way to the opposite end of the hall.'

This is what I was dreading but didn't think I would have to perform the task so early. This was a reason why I had asked for Fiona's help in the first place. I had worked on it at home but made no progress since Fiona's visit.

When Dobby was called, Dad guided me towards Fiona. She held Dobby while we made our way to the other side of the hall.

'Okay, Billy, when you're ready, call him to you,' Fiona said.

She released Dobby, and I called his name. He started walking towards me but ran to other dogs.

'Ah, I'm sorry,' I said.

'It's okay,' the woman to my left said. 'He's only coming to talk to Katie.'

'This one is going to need a little work,' Fiona said, re-trieving Dobby for another try. 'This time, call him again, but a little more firmly.'

I did as she said, but he did it again.

The hall burst out in laughter at Dobby's second attempt when he got a little closer but ran to the other side of the hall.

'That was a little better,' she assured me. 'We'll try once more.'

Again, I called him towards me. And again, he broke off to see dogs on the other side. All of the dogs were a lot better at re-call than Dobby. But they could see. It was going to take longer for me.

'It'll take time,' Fiona said, finishing up for the session. 'Work on the same tasks for next week, guys.'

Because the next session was the day after bonfire night, Fiona warned us about fireworks and to be vigilant with our dog. She suggested getting the dog used to the sound of fireworks by accessing a platform from which you can play the sounds. The idea was to play the sounds at a low volume and meanwhile play with your dog while to distract it, increasing the volume a little at a time. I took her advice and did as she said.

I wanted to make sure he was both fed and walked before class. This way, he wouldn't need his exercise afterwards. But was a walk a good idea before class? And so close to fireworks night?

Dad had barely reached the bottom of the car park with Dobby when I heard the first rocket. I prayed Dobby took it well and that they didn't affect him. When Dad returned with Dobby half-an-hour later, I asked him how Dobby reacted.

'He gave a little jump when the first firework sounded,' Dad said.

'Was he okay after that?'

'Aye, he stopped and looked at them.'

The next session was pretty much the same as the first;

walks around the hall, interacting with other dogs, the dreaded re-call, and Dad in command. The re-call was something I worked on at home with little effect. It was no different at classes! He still ran to talk to other dogs. Fiona suggested I bring a favourite toy along next time to encourage him—or cover myself in cheese.

Similar to re-call, *sit*, *lie down* and *stand* were more crucial commands to teach the dogs. Again, Dad took charge of these tasks while I watched. What was the point in me being there! I could sit at home on a comfy couch rather than have a sore bum on a plastic seat.

And like the attentiveness task, the dog didn't have to be far in front of you—a lead's length was enough. He wasn't bad at these, especially sit and lie down. But he was reluctant to stand when asked. In fact, he preferred to lie down. Fiona walked around the hall checking on the progress of each dog. She came to us last.

'Did you walk and feed him before class?' she asked, looking at Dobby lying down on his side.

Dobby didn't lie on his front the way he was supposed to. When I had taught him to lie down, he lay on his side. So, that's what he got used to when he heard that command. He always sat when told but rarely stayed standing when commanded.

'Aye, we did feed him,' Dad replied, fingering the lead handle.

'He's shattered,' she said. 'Don't feed and walk him before next week's class. He's too tired to do the training.'

Both Dad and I turned to each other, faces flushed. While

I preferred Dobby to eat before class, Dad didn't stop me. He didn't get everything right! We took her advice and didn't feed and walk him before classes. More fireworks were going off when Dobby got home. We left the back door open, and he sat looking at them light up the night sky. They didn't seem to bother him.

Chapter 13

MY ROCK

It was important for me that Dobby learned to walk with his dad. I'd been taking Dobby to different places with Mum during November, but some were more difficult than others. A place where I wanted to walk him, and thought would be simple enough, was Billow Ness, a beach alongside the golf course.

On stormy days the sea gallops across the rocks sending seaweed and sand to smash against the sea wall. It's like claps of thunder as waves bang against the harbour, spraying sand across the road like a firework display. On quieter days the lapping waves dance like dolphins up the beach on the shores of Billow Ness, a sandy bay on the Fife Coastal Path.

When the tide is out, you can walk from Billow Ness right along the sea wall to Anstruther. My friends and I got caught out by the rising tide a few times, trying to outwit the tidal monster opening its wide frothy jaws as if it would swallow us whole.

I can almost picture the dark outline of Johnny Doo's rock, as I sat in the car at the shore in the middle of November. My hazy vision prevents this. I wanted and needed places where I was able to walk my dog. I knew walking him was going to be one of my biggest challenges.

My first time in mid-September was interesting to say the least. It is less than a minute's walk for an able-bodied person to the playpark behind the houses of Dreelside, a popular place for dog walkers. Beyond the park is a nature reserve called Dreel Meadows, which has hedgerows, trees and a stream called The Dreel Burn.

I tried this short distance to begin with. We had two Dobby leads—a leather one for Mum and Dad to use and a retractable one for me. I thought a retractable lead would be better as I had no idea how he would cope with my crutches. This way, I could thread my belt through the handle and adjust the length to suit before locking in the clip. However, I had to catch the little bugger first!

If he saw his lead, he ran away. If he ran laps around the garden, it was impossible. If he ran inside, it was possible. If he ran into a corner, it was easy. If he ran into his cage—it was job done. With Mum's help we got the lead on and began our walk. However, we didn't get far; he lay down on a grassy area just before the park, refusing to go any further so we returned to the house. I was surprised how much easier it was going back, but delighted he walked with me.

'Well, that's going to work, Mum' I said when we got home.

'Aye, that wasn't bad. One of your dad's customers told him it's not a big deal if he struggles to walk at first,' she replied. 'The main thing is toilet training.'

'I know, Mum, but he needs to get used to walking with me.'

'She said their hips are still developing and they can have problems later in life.'

I later learned that his hips would seize up from lack of exercise or slower walks. Puppies need good, long walks so that their hips have a chance to develop. I didn't want my dog to have hip problems, so I let Mum and Dad walk Dobby for a while before I took him out again.

~~~

It was important Dobby walked with a collar and lead and without pulling. The breeder advised me to keep his collar on, so he'd get used to wearing it. I wasn't fussed for a harness. He was up to date with vaccinations and allowed out, but he wouldn't go at first. Why was this?

Since I had got Dobby, the weather had been alternating between glorious sunshine and torrential rain. Dad tried to pop round to walk him each morning before starting his fish round—but Dobby wouldn't go. Mum carried out walking duties later, but he still wouldn't go. Especially if it was pouring. He got as far as the back fence and wouldn't move. He didn't want to go without me, but I insisted they persevere. Dobby needed to learn his main walks were with his granny, grandad or both. And, eventually, their perseverance paid off.

He was nearly five months old before I started walking him regularly—and I wanted to take him to Dreel Meadows.

Despite me being adamant about Dobby not wearing a harness; Dad came in one night clutching a bag. It was pouring with rain, and he came to walk Dobby. His neighbour lent him a harness and coat for Dobby. She thought this would
~~~

be better and wouldn't choke him. He was legally required to have his collar on outside but how would a harness benefit a dog when he didn't need one? Dad didn't have the final say. I was adamant he was not wearing a coat, but trying the harness wouldn't harm him. Dobby wouldn't move the first time we put it on—not even around the house. If he wasn't happy with it on in the house, how was he going to walk with one outside? He managed a few yards before Mum took it off. He walked fine after that.

Access from Dreelside to Dreel Meadows is either from a gentle decline from the road, or a flight of steep steps from the park. Both lead to the burn. We started at the slope as we thought the steps would be too tricky. I was more famil-iar with this route as my friends and I used to play there. I remember a large grassy area which we used to cut through to get to the main road.

A play scheme ran every summer at my old high school. We took part in all kinds of activities and one of those was a game called, 'Tracking.' Our team left chalk arrows for the other team to follow. The team leader took us across the main road then across the grass to an old footbridge over the burn. That was a long way for me, hampered with cerebral palsy.

Once we reached the footbridge, the leader told us to wait while he crossed it. He drew a large X, then re-joined us. But instead of taking us across the bridge, he led us onto the bank under it. We all sniggered when we heard the other team's feet thundering above us. They were baffled to find the X, but no sign of us. We stayed hidden for a few moments, until our laughter gave us away.

Mum and I planned to walk across the bridge, over the grass, behind the industrial estate and along the old railway bridge back to Dreelside. But we encountered an unexpected problem. We couldn't take the shortcut. I hadn't been there for years and didn't know it was now fenced off. Instead, we went back the way we had come and made our way to the steps under the old railway bridge. All the time, Dobby's nose was to the ground.

'Come on, Dobby, leave it,' I said.

'He's just sniffing,' Mum said. 'There'll be hundreds of new smells for him down here.'

'I know, Mum, but the quicker I stop him doing that the better.'

'But that's what dogs do.'

'Fiona said to cut that out. She said to keep your dog focused on you. He needs to walk with me and not to sniff every two seconds.'

'I'm not sure how you'll manage that. Dogs like to know who's been here.'

He still walked beside me. We reached the steps, and I was curious to know how we would cope. Unclipping the lead, I let Dobby hop ahead while I struggled my way up. He was standing waiting at each landing. When I reached him, I stroked him while I caught my breath.

'Clever boy,' I said, before letting him hop ahead to the next landing.

An able-bodied person would have taken ten minutes to do that walk. It took me forty-five.

I found the Dreel Meadows too tiring so decided to stick

to simpler walks. One of these walks was the first one I had tried. But I, with Mum's help, managed to get Dobby further and further. Walking Dobby up the park was a lot flatter and not as tiring.

'C'mon Dobby.' I pulled on his lead.

Dobby wouldn't budge if he saw something. It was usually another dog, or cat.

'C'mon Dobby,' I said again, but for as small as he was, he stood, solid.

'Why is he not moving, Mum?' I asked, feebly tugging the lead.

'Oh, he's spotted a seagull,' she said, taking her eyes off her phone.

It reminded me of a seagull trying to get into my living room through the window one day. I still hear the squawks of the gulls as they swoop and soar, attempting to snatch someone's fish and chips while they sit on the prom. The deafening sound seems to have multiplied in the last few years.

'C'mon Dobby,' I said. 'It's only a seagull, you silly bugger. It'll probably eat you. It's bigger than you.'

With Mum's help, I managed to pull him away from his trance.

Dobby was now getting used to walking with his dad. He had grown to know when it was time for a walk. He grew out of running away from his lead. When I dangled it and called, 'walkies,' he came to me, lay down and presented his neck. He also learned quickly to get out of my way when I approached, standing up then moving aside before following as I shuffled around the house. He was reluctant to walk when it rained, and he still didn't like anything on his body, whether it be a harness or a raincoat. But he didn't mind a towel.

At Billow Ness, once out of the car, Dobby waited patiently as I attached his lead to my belt. We stood as I had another gaze towards Johnny Doo's rock, waiting on Mum getting things from the car. Sliding my treat pouch through my belt, we were ready to go.

With Mum's help I had begun walking Dobby more, and to more places. If the journey was too far for me, Mum took us in the car. One of these journeys was to Kilrenny Common—a neighbouring village to the east of Anstruther and Cellardyke. Kilrenny Common, or the Common as the locals call it, has always been a popular spot for picnics, walks and dog walking. I hadn't set foot in the place for several years but, despite having little sight, the Common brought back so many memories to me. The furthest back I can remember was when I attended, with a group of other children, a school trip to Kilrenny Common. I must have been about ten or eleven years old when I attended a Busy Bodies club at the East Neuk Centre. It was Halloween and we'd gone to Kilrenny for a scare-fest. I wasn't able to run around the woods like the other children, so the youth club leader carried me on his back, running in and out of the woods, scaring everyone with our masks.

Another good thing about the Common was the family gatherings. Our parents held barbecues there and, with some encouragement, got everyone to play a game of rounders. Again, I wasn't able to run so, one of my uncles picked me up on the way round. When we weren't hanging around our parents, my cousins and I were playing down by the burn, dropping sticks in the water and watching them float away.

I remember the familiar crunch of tyres on gravel as Mum parked the car. I slid myself out of the car while Mum got Dobby out. She handed me my belt and retractable lead while she put on Dobby's collar.

Once we were both ready, I clipped the lead on, took the crutches from Mum and off we went. She had to walk in front, as I had no idea which direction I was going. However, after clearing the gravel, my feet found grass. I instantly heard running water to my north. I heard the mooing of cows and bleating of sheep in the distance to the far north-east. And a new sound of clucking chickens and roosters to the south. The grass was very squishy and soft as we made our way around the Common.

It had rained heavily a couple of days earlier, but the ground was still muddy. I wasn't able to explore the whole common with Dobby, like I once used to, but a short walk around the grassy area would do.

I unclipped the catch on the retractable, allowing Dobby to explore his surroundings—retracting the lead back in if I caught him sniffing too much. He caught sight of other dogs now and again and pulled towards them, my crutches slipping in the mushy ground. If another owner didn't mind, I let Dobby say hello. We met the old driving instructor walking his labrador. Again, Dobby wanted to say hello.

Walking Dobby up the Common was more difficult than I anticipated as he wanted to investigate all of the new smells, sounds and distractions. The driving instructor assured us it would get easier, but it might take a couple of years. He also put his hand over his dog's snout to demonstrate they grow out of biting. My dog had already stopped. Subsequent visits to the Common did get easier but for this one I was tired and needed back to the car.

We began our walk towards Billow Ness swings—which was at the top of the long, sloping road adjacent to the beach on the left and the golf course on the right. A high wire fence also ran along the side of the golf course. Where the high fence stopped, another one started on the left, preventing anyone from falling onto the rocks below. A steep thirty-foot grassy hill led up to the second hole.

A group of friends used to play on the hill, which is still a popular place for sledging when we have snow, which is rare being so close to the east coast. If you know how, you can push off from the top, navigate your way down, avoid the two fences and land on the beach.

Mum, Dobby and I made our way out of the car park towards the barrier, which had been there as long as I could remember. Although the road was wide enough for a car, they were prohibited from using it. Ignoring my own advice to keep Dobby close, I let the lead out, allowing him to wander in front. His instinct was to pull to the left, as his granny or grandad often took him there for a run on the beach. He learned to love the beach but not the sea because he doesn't like water.

'C'mon, Dobby, this way,' I said, as I gave the lead a tug. 'The beach is for another time.'

He obliged and ran ahead, in front of us. I did not want

my dog to get into the habit of sniffing. But letting the lead in and out was allowing him to do just that. I often caught up with him, as he was too busy investigating a new scent. I knew Jack Russells were bred to find and get rid of vermin, but I was determined to train him as a pet. Although it is in a Jack Russell's nature to hunt, I tried to stop him from doing so.

The walk took ages with Dobby sniffing everything. He almost sniffed his way off the cliff. Luckily, Mum caught him on time. I heard Fiona's voice in my head.

'It is important to prevent your dog from sniffing. If you don't, then it will be difficult to stop your dog while out on walks. Keep your dog by your side and tell him off if he pulls to the side. Give him a reward if he stops.'

I followed her advice and drew the lead in closer to my side and clipped the lead shut. We continued up the hill, tugging the lead if Dobby pulled towards something, telling him to leave it, whatever it was. I was conscious of onlookers from the large bay windows of the clubhouse watching my slow progress, but we made it.

Standing next to the swings, I looked in the direction to where Johnny Doo's rock should be and remembered years ago when I christened Johnny Doo's Pulpit as 'My Rock.' I was eleven years old when I first made the climb. Most days in the summer of 1993, along with my cousins and my brother, I attempted the ascent. It never crossed our minds how dangerous this was; we just wanted to reach the top. There was also the problem of getting cut off, as the base became submerged under water at high tide. We always climbed up when the tide was going out but remained alert and kept an eye out when the tide turned.

You can see the whole world from the top of my rock—or to an eleven-year-old that's what it seemed like. If you stood at the top now, you would see that a number of landmarks have disappeared from view since I was younger. The Craw's Nest Hotel and Chalmers Church were two of the most visible landmarks of Anstruther from a distance. Some say the great fire which burned Chalmers Church to the ground on the 10th of May 1991 was deliberately lit. The tall spire could be seen for miles by fisherman as they made their way home to their loved ones, but now it's a block of flats. The Craw's Nest was a thriving hotel with fifty rooms and accommodated many visitors to the town, but was bought over and shortly went into decline before being knocked down to be replaced with luxury apartments for the elderly.

However, the Pulpit Rock at Johnny Doo's still remains a significant feature of the landscape of Anstruther. After some research, I found that a covenanter preacher stood on top of the rock, where a single rusty pole still juts out, to address illegally the congregation below, in opposition to the interference of the Stuart kings.

I remember watching the waves crash against the rocks while the rest of the group ran around dodging the spray, which hissed and spat at them like an angry cobra. I would sit for what felt like hours enjoying the salty sea air and the soft blissfulness of the warm breeze on my face while the others played. I couldn't join in, of course. Even getting up here was an achievement for me with cerebral palsy. I was always determined to make the climb independently but was happy to know my brother was by my side until I reached the top.

Johnny Doo's Pulpit is still there of course, but the landmark has almost disappeared from my view, as my eyesight has deteriorated so much since childhood. Even with assistance my visual impairment makes approaching my rock too dangerous. Disappointed I can no longer see Johnny Doo's, the three of us headed back to the car.

'Your Dad and me have been thinking,' Mum began. 'We feel that we should train Dobby for you.'

My pulse quickened. My chest tightened. And I let out a heavy sigh.

'No, I don't think so,' I said.

'But people train dogs for other people,' Mum said.

'Aye, but I'm different. We've been through this. I need to train him.'

'Plenty of dogs are trained for disabled people.'

'Dobby's different, Mum. If you and Dad train him, he'll answer to you both and not me. I need to do it.'

'Okay, if that's what you want.'

'Aye, it is,' I finished.

As I slid myself into the car, I gazed once more in the direction of Johnny Doo's and I wished I could return once more to that spot on the top of the rock. I will never again manage to do so, but it's not to say Dobby won't.

Chapter 14

UNCLE WEH

We had my cousin and her husband's 30th birthday party to attend in late October, and despite Dad insisting Dobby shouldn't be left on his own, we had to leave him. The venue wasn't far, so one of us could nip home to check on Dobby. I wasn't going to stay long, anyway.

Mum, Dad, Mya and Mikey left my house around seven and walked the short distance, Dad pushing me in my chair. We took Dobby with us, and when everyone had arrived at the party, Dad walked him home again. Dad wheeled me home about ten. Dad and I made sure Dobby was comfortable before Dad left again for the party.

My back was turned for a few seconds when I realised Dobby wasn't beside me. Dad had left one of the kitchen seats out and I found Dobby, quite the thing, curled up on the seat. If the hairy dog could jump up there already, it wouldn't be long before he could jump onto anything he wanted. I had to make sure all chairs were tucked in or at least the one I sat on was far enough from the table. However, on the chair, underneath the table became one of his go-to places for security. I often found him there if I was looking for him.

<div style="text-align: center;">~~~</div>

The end of November approached, and the month had been calm and mild. It did rain heavily at times. This discouraged Dobby from going outside to do his business. He was improving with his toilet training but when it rained, I still found the odd puddle on the living room floor but not so often on the kitchen floor. One of my dad's customers suggested we try an anti-odour spray on the areas after wiping up his mess. I had hoped this would prevent him from peeing on the floor. But it didn't. I was spraying the stuff everywhere—even on the coffee table, where he often jumped up to look out the window. I squeezed lemon juice on areas where he chewed but this didn't work either.

Dobby seemed to like chewing corners of things. Modern thinking suggests chewing is a normal canine pastime which is enjoyable for the dog and keeps the jaws and teeth in good shape. I had my doubts. Sometimes I felt he did it to annoy me.

One day, when I had a friend round, he was in the toilet with his dog (he often took her with him) when I heard crunching. I thought it was his dog chewing an empty toilet roll tube. The crunching became louder. I was unaware Dobby was hunkered down, chewing the corner of my living room wall—leaving a mound of plasterboard. After this incident, I had to keep a close eye on him.

Sometime in early November my friend suggested that I buy a Flat Fox. What was a Flat Fox? Basically, it's a dog toy resembling, yes, a flat fox, which dogs love to play with and chew, but without harming the dog. I couldn't find a Flat

Fox, so I got a squirrel instead. The poor squirrel's ears were bitten off in no time. But it took a long time to destroy the toy completely. Dobby and I played with this toy a lot. I sat in the middle of the settee and teased Dobby with it. I threw it behind my back, and he jumped for it. I whipped it away before he grabbed it. Repeating the game, I carried on until he tired. I tempted him with the same toy to encourage him away from the wall. It didn't work. Instead, I picked him up and held him to my chest gently telling him it was wrong.

Mum sometimes looked after Dobby at my house so that I could visit the pub to see friends and have a couple of pints. I told her she would need to play with Dobby for a bit and use the Flat Squirrel. I promised I wouldn't be long, and I never was. However, in late November, I decided to venture further afield and visit my friends in St Andrews. Mum and Dad kept Dobby that night. My eyes welled up when Dad lifted him up to my level to give his dad kisses.

'Be a good boy for Granny and Grandad,' I said, stroking his head before Dad took him away. The bus journey felt like hours. It had been the first time I travelled a distance on the bus since getting Dobby. I got off across from the Criterion. I heard clinking of empty glasses being cleared from tables as I approached. Although they sold my favourite lager, it tasted like vinegar. I pictured Dobby sitting whining at the top of Mum and Dad's garden waiting for his dad to come home.

I used my long cane to find my way to Blackhorns, a modernised old-style diner which served burgers and hot dogs. A strong whiff of fried food escape from the vent above me as I fumbled for the door handle. I'd been to this place once, and it had been full of students sitting at high tables and a long queue waiting to be served. No one occupied seats that night. I had a hotdog and chips. I could hardly eat my food for retching. Every mouthful took an eternity to disappear down my gullet, instantly threatening to come straight back up. My friend passed as I sparked up a cigarette outside. I told him I wouldn't be long. I thought a cigarette would calm my nerves, but I couldn't smoke for choking. I did relax a little once I made it to the pub. Having a drink and a laugh with my friends took my mind off being away from Dobby for a bit, but when my taxi arrived to take me home, my anxiety levels returned greater than ever.

I'd lived on my own for fifteen years and was used to my own space. So why was going into an empty house different? I no longer had an empty space. Dobby had filled that gap in my life. I had company for the first time in years. I had a dog to share my life with. I opened his cage door tensing at the excitement of Dobby pouncing on me to lick my face. Finding a slobbery toy, I picked it up, smelled it and put it down. I sat on the couch, pressing my face into where Dobby's little body lay curled up beside me. Finding his discarded Flat Squirrel on the floor, I picked it up and took it to bed with me. I lay his toy beside my face. A part of Dobby took away the emptiness. Dad brought him back the following day around noon and I lay on the settee waiting for him. When he found me, he jumped on top of me and rolled around; he had missed his dad as much as I missed him. I swore that I wouldn't go to St Andrews again until he was a lot older.

~~~
~~~

Usually, Mum or Dad took Dobby out for his walks, but they, along with my auntie and uncle, go on an annual weekend trip to Aberdeen for some Christmas shopping with friends of the family. So, my brother, Michael had to walk him instead. This was the first time I was completely on my own with Dobby. Before they left on the Friday, Dad came to assemble my Christmas tree. Once up, the lights were too tempting for Dobby as they danced around in front of his curious eyes.

'See you Sunday,' Dad said, leaving us to it.

'Aye, have a nice time.' Dobby and I watched Dad head to the door.

'Your brother will be up for Dobby's walks,' he added, before departing.

The minute he left; Dobby headed back to the tree. He pressed his nose on a bulb and the tree shook. He backed away. He tried again. The same happened.

'Come away from the tree, Dobby,' I said.

He turned his head, acknowledging me but returned to the tree.

'Dobby, come away from there,' I said again.

With no joy, I lowered myself onto my knees and crawled towards him. When I slid my hand down his snout, I discovered it wasn't the lights he was interested in, it was the decorations Dad had hung on the branches. Moving his snout aside, I said again…

It took a few attempts but once he knew this habit was bad, he stopped. There were other areas of the living room he became interested in. For example, the stuffed Santa Claus which sat on the coffee table. The little Christmas ornaments

Dad placed on my TV unit. And the jangly bells I thought were far out of reach on top of the picture of my niece and nephew.

It was no surprise that Dobby could reach the Christmas decoration on top of the picture. He'd been able to jump onto the settee after a few weeks, and I didn't want to prevent him from doing so. I wanted him to be able to leap up beside me, or onto the settee, unaided.

Dobby and I sat on the settee waiting for Michael. We listened to the storm raging. No one should put a pet out in such weather, but he needed his exercise.

I contemplated bracing the storm and taking Dobby myself. We would head to the pub, have a couple of pints and come home again. This would be his walk. But I decided against the idea.

The wind whistled through the branches of the tree outside my living room window. The tree shook its long finger-like branches in protest. The rain came down in torrents as it spat and sprayed the window.

I played as much with Dobby as I could, but the spritely pup could play for hours given the chance. However, I had also learned from Jean Donaldson's book that it is important to teach your dog when playtime is finished. Short commands should be enough. For example, I chose to use the phrase, *that's enough play.* This is easier said than done with an energetic Jack Russell. There were many toys scattered around the kitchen and living room now, but he preferred some to others—mostly the ones he could destroy. I persisted with tuggy toys, and he loved a good tussle with his dad. I flung him around the floor, his teeth attached to one end as my hand grabbed the other. But he often preferred my end of the toy. It didn't matter how much I tried; I could not get Dobby to let go of a toy when I told him. I had to put rope toys away when finished or he sat chewing them and they often got caught in his throat.

Dobby's ears pricked up at a noise outside. It was a vehicle door slamming. This was something I hadn't picked up on during the time I'd stayed in this house. But once Dobby had come into my life, I became aware of every car door slam. His little head popped up every time he heard a car, van, or lorry. I had to start saying to him, 'It's not for you.' But this time it was. Michael arrived through the door like the Titanic steering into the iceberg.

'Dobbinens,' Michael yelled.

He knows his name is Dobby. However, he has adopted additional names, such as Dobbs. Cool Dobbinator—a play on the lyrics, *Smooth Operator* by Sade. Dobbinens being the name we use the most.

'C'mon then Dobbinens,' he said, as Dobby raced to greet him, his tail swishing furiously.

'Weh,' Michael said, rubbing Dobby's head and body.

Dobby doesn't know my brother's name is Michael. His name to Dobby is Uncle Weh. It's the way Michael greets him. It's his way of showing affection for Dobby. Every time he sees him, he says, 'weh.' The name stuck. Ever since, my brother was known as Uncle Weh.

According to *Barkersize.com*, a website detailing dogs and their habits, a Jack Russell should be walked for up to or more than thirty minutes, twice a day. This wasn't easy for me; I preferred someone to walk him for the recommended time. Dobby released his energy by playing with me in the house.

While Dobby was away with Uncle Weh, it allowed me to relax and have a rest for half-an-hour. However, this wasn't to be. They had barely left when… I heard a door slam. Seconds later, another door slammed. 'He must have taken the van,' I thought, as I checked the time. He'd only been away for fifteen minutes but at least he took Dobby out for me.

Michael loves Dobby. He was also influential in helping to source a dog. Initially, when I was interested in a Jack Russell, he looked for people who were selling them. He could only find people selling bitches. He knew I wanted a dog, so he continued searching. Michael walked Dobby regularly. Unfortunately, Dad discouraged him. One night, Michael was walking Dobby and me home from our parents' when Dobby wouldn't budge. Dad was watching from the top of the garden path. He was keeping an eye on us. There was no need, as Michael was more than capable. But Dobby wouldn't move because he saw his grandad at the top of the garden. He often wouldn't move, because he expected everyone to go. But his grandad wasn't coming. It wasn't a big deal.

Uncle Weh visited again towards the end of December to assemble a new sideboard unit. To stop Dobby from stealing anymore DVDs, I thought that if I had a much larger unit, I could store all of my films away. My brother was a skilled joiner—one of the best in the business. A lot of people, including me, praised his professionalism. I knew he wouldn't take long in putting it together. Dobby was curious to see what Uncle Weh was up to, so he kept investigating When the drill sounded, he bolted to the kitchen.

A few days after Uncle Weh assembled my unit, my friend and his dog were around again, and I ushered Dobby to the back door for a pee. Opening the door, we discovered it was lashing down. Dobby had second thoughts. He padded to the place he knew underneath the Christmas tree. It sounded like the biggest pee he had ever done. I, my friend and his dog stared at Dobby. He must have sensed something was wrong and it was like a switch—it clicked, and Dobby never peed in the house again on purpose. If he did, it was an accident. From that day on, *Underneath the Tree*, by Kelly Clarkson became one of my favourite Christmas songs.

DOBBY WORLD

Dobby chilling out with a friend

One small puppy against the world

"It wasn't me."

Dobby with his dad.

Chapter 15

SLEEPLESS NIGHTS

After pacing my flat all afternoon, slouching on the couch, shuffling around the house, phone in hand—the screen finally lit up. Voiceover announced Provost Vet calling.

'How's Dobby?' I asked, not waiting for pleasantries.

I gripped my mobile tight as I awaited the reply.

'Dobby's awake now, so you can collect him,' the veterinary nurse said.

'How did his procedure go?' I asked, praying there were no complications.

'It went well,' she replied.

'That's good then.' I relaxed my fingers. 'I'll let Mum know, and we'll pick him up shortly.'

The main reason the breeder sold Dobby to me was that I would get him neutered at the earliest opportunity. To prevent me having an out-of-control Jack Russell, it was advised I should make plans to get him neutered when he was six- months old. I booked him in for the middle of January. It meant he would be in, operated on, and healed in time to take him, along with Mum and Dad to celebrate my thirty-eighth birthday in the Royal. This would be pushing it, but I was hopeful.

I had allowed Mum to take Dobby for his operation. I couldn't face going and leaving the vet's without him. If he was to fall out with anyone for leaving him, it wasn't going to be me! Besides, he had to be dropped off at eight o clock. I was studying for a master's degree at the same time and a support worker came to assist me at eight thirty. I was happy to collect him with Mum. She phoned me after she'd dropped him off and explained that the operation was going to be a little more expensive than I was quoted. The reason for this was, that on examining Dobby's testicles, one hadn't dropped into its sac. We had an idea this might be the case, as Dad and I handled Dobby's body regularly, making sure everything was in working order.

'It was fifty pounds more,' Mum said on the phone. 'I didn't check with you, because I thought you'd be okay with that.'

'No, that's fine, Mum.'

Before Dobby's operation, the nurse had given us leaflets on the neutering procedure. I'd asked her if she could email a digital copy. She obliged, and the email was in my inbox before I left the vet's. I was able to read all the information before Dobby's operation and I wasn't surprised they needed to go deeper to retrieve the hidden testicle.

On the other hand, Dobby's breeder had showed Dad Dobby's marbles, as she called them, and assured us they were in perfect working order. We believe my Jack Russell had been reserved for someone else who had turned him down because they wanted the dog with two healthy working testicles. However, the surgery was done, and all was good.

I always spend Christmas Day at Mum and Dad's—a tradition for as long as I can remember. Dobby's first Christmas was also spent at his granny and grandad's. In previous years, my auntie and Mum took year about but with Auntie Julie's growing family, it got a bit much. There was now a new member of our family. Dad usually picks me up around eleven to take me down, and once there, that's me for the day.

Before I got Dobby, Dad dropped my parcels off on Christmas Eve. They lay there until morning. Despite Mum and Dad believing I opened them before I went to bed, I never did. Besides, I usually went to the pub every Christmas, came home and watched *Santa Claus the Movie*. This year was different! Dad did not drop my presents off this time, as Dobby still had a tendency to tear things apart. My presents were waiting for me at Mum and Dad's, along with Dobby's present.

A number of Dobby's toys lay scattered across my house now. Anything to prevent him chewing the furniture. He preferred some toys to others. I kept an eye on what he chewed and didn't. I put tuggy toys away after using them—especially rope toys. If I left them lying around, they got stuck in his teeth, or his throat. He wasn't happy when I took them away. Plastic toys were another thing I had to watch for. He loved anything plastic, and not just toys. I resorted to buying hard unbreakable toys even a German Shepherd would struggle to break.

His granny bought him a Woof Glider for Christmas. She saw an advert for it on JML Direct. The Woof Glider has a flat base design and soft rubber bumpers, which won't harm your dog's teeth and prevents it from bouncing. It's meant to help your dog to release energy by pouncing on it. It's also meant to glide across any surface, but all it did was mark my mum's vinyl. Mum bought one for my house and it marked my laminate. Dobby wasn't interested in the thing, anyway.

~~~

I have been a member of a blind charity called BASE (Blind, Activities, Support Events) since 2009, and took the post of chairman in 2018. BASE is a charity which encourages blind and partially sighted people to be less isolated and attend monthly events on the first Thursday of each month. I didn't want to give this up when I got Dobby.

The October event was to visit the Deep Sea World in North Queensferry, Fife. I always looked forward to each event whether I was interested in where we were going or not. I liked to get out for a while. Mum checked on Dobby and let him out for a bit while I was away. But the second I left home, until the time I got back, I thought about him. I should have been interested in the sharks, marine life and seal display, but I wasn't. Retail therapy isn't my thing, but I asked my volunteer guide to take me to the shop. They had squeaky shark toys which I thought would be a good toy for Dobby. But it was plastic! It was ruined in no time.

~~~

Mum and I went to collect Dobby from the vet late afternoon. On arrival, the nurse explained what we already knew. She beckoned us through to the treatment room. I stood as stiff as a board, as she disappeared through the back.

'Here he is then,' the nurse announced, opening the door a few minutes later.

My knees weakened when Dobby came padding through, his little tail swishing through the air at the sight of us.

I held out a hand for him to lick. He crawled up my leg to reach my outstretched fingers. Mum picked him up so I could cuddle him to my neck.

'He's already had a lick at his stitches,' the nurse went on. 'We'll have to put a cone on him.'

A cone, otherwise known as an Elizabethan Collar, is designed to fit over your dog's head and neck to prevent it from licking or scratching a wound. It ties around the neck, so it doesn't come off. It looked more like a lampshade than a cone. She explained to Mum how to put the cone on, as this would be something I wouldn't manage.

'He's had something to eat,' she continued. 'I'll give you a few tins to take away with you and only give him this for a few days.'

I was reluctant to give him the food, as he'd only just start-ed to eat and enjoy the food I put down to him. Dobby had been a fussy eater since I got him, but the Hills prescription diet she gave us to take away was the preferred food to give your dog after an operation. She made an appointment for us to come back a few days later for a check-up.

Dobby and I went straight to Mum and Dad's for tea when we got home. Mum put some of the food prescribed by the vet down to him and he wolfed it down. I wondered how he would cope with eating and drinking while his cone was on. We also had strict instructions to walk him for only ten minutes a day. His ten minutes was from Mum and Dad's to my house. That's how long I take to walk up the road, anyway. It was a long day for both of us, so I put him to bed when we got home, but I had concerns. He couldn't get his mouth far enough into his bowl to drink his water. Dad had to fill several bowls to the brim to make sure he had plenty. And how was he going to fit in his cage with his cone?

But after a little manoeuvring around, he managed to settle himself into a comfortable position. Reaching my hand inside, I felt around to see how he lay. But his head was facing towards the wall, away from me again. I had dreaded the day of his procedure and had anticipated both his and my discomfort. I couldn't play with him. I couldn't cuddle him. The only thing I could do was slide my hand under the cone and give his head a rub. As much as I couldn't bear to see my little boy this way, it was for the best.

~~~

It was almost a month since Dobby had peed in the house, so I introduced him to the other rooms. He would bolt past me if I hadn't closed the living room door properly and he sneaked by me if I wasn't quick enough. This was something I tried to cut out. He had to learn that I was the boss. However, it was his house too, and I had to allow him through eventually. I rarely allowed him into my bedroom at night.

I'd made plans to sleep in the living room before Dobby's operation because I didn't know what to expect. I thought he
~~~

might have to be beside me at night. I tried to familiarise him with sleeping somewhere other than his cage. Dad prepared a sleeping bag on the settee for me. He also moved Dobby's bed and his water bowl into the living room. He told me where he placed his bowl and to be careful not to knock it over. I flicked through the Sky channels until I found something to watch. I settled on *Us*—a movie my volunteer had taken me to see at the cinema a few months earlier.

I couldn't get comfortable. I couldn't sleep. Where was he? What he was up to when I slept! I thought he would jump up beside me, but he didn't. He had no interest in his bed, or his water. I lay until after midnight before deciding to go to my bed. I took a risk. I prayed that Dobby behaved himself on his own.

The main concern I had was the corner of the wall where he kept chewing. Dad had taped it up, but Dobby often pulled the tape off with his teeth. I thought everything was in order when I went through around six the next morning, but I was wrong. The tape was off the wall. It was wrapped around his teeth. This wasn't going to work; he would have to stay in his cage.

I didn't let Dobby out of my sight, or earshot rather, after his operation. I let him out the back for the toilet and had a cigarette while he was out. I listened out for him while I watched telly. However, a couple of days after his opera-tion, I heard constant licking. Where was it coming from? I hadn't shut the living room door properly. I rushed into the bedroom and followed the sound. He had managed to angle his cone and body so he could get to his wound. Terrified he might have reached his stitches, I called Mum. She arrived in minutes and inspected the wound.

'It's a bit red,' she said, studying the area.

'D'you think we should take him to the vet?' I asked, gulping back tears.

'Aye, I think so,' she replied. 'It'll be okay.' She rested her head on my shoulder. ''We'll get him sorted.' She re-attached his cone.

'I hope so,' I said, biting my lower lip.

The vet asked us to bring him in. We were back in the consultation room a short time later.

'Yes, that looks a bit nasty,' the nurse said, examining Dobby. 'We're going to have to put a bigger cone on you, little man,' she continued. 'And give you something to clear that up.'

'It'll be okay,' Mum said, laying a hand on my shoulder.

The nurse disappeared again and returned with a much larger cone and medication.

'Okay,' she began. 'Give him these antibiotics with his food and rub this cream around his wound twice daily.'

'Will he be, okay?' I asked.

'He should be,' she assured me. 'The medication should do the trick. And the larger cone will stop him from reaching his wound.'

Both Mum and I nodded.

'Now let's get this on you, wee man,' the nurse began again. 'These cones are usually for bigger dogs like German Shepherds, but we can't have you licking your wound now.'

We had a new appointment to come back on the Friday, which was only a week since his operation. It also meant

I would have to give my birthday celebrations a miss. But Dobby was more important. With the new cone around his neck, we thanked the woman and headed out. Not only was Dobby's new cone bigger, but it was also heavier. I winced every time I heard the cone clatter against, the floor. The walls. And even the door on our way out.

I needed Mum and Dad's assistance more than ever. I wondered if it was such a good idea owning a dog after all. Had I set my ambitions too high and perhaps raising a Jack Russell independently *was* beyond my ability. His new cone was too big for him to eat or drink. It had to be removed for mealtimes—something I couldn't do on my own and had to rely on Mum or Dad to come round every day to feed him.

'I want to feed my own dog,' I moaned one day.

'You will,' Mum offered, in her soft tone. 'It's only for a wee while.'

'I know, but…'

'It's fine. We'll be here to help, and you'll get your dog back when he's all healed.'

'I hope it's not long then,' I said, a tear running down my cheek.

Dobby was able to fit in his cage with his small cone, but he couldn't with this one. Where was he going to sleep? There was only one solution. He would have to sleep in my room beside me. I had planned, one day, he would get to sleep in my bedroom, but I didn't think he was ready yet. Because he curls up beside me on the couch, Dad thought that would be his bed eventually, or at the foot of my bed.

We prepared Dobby for different arrangements. But would

different arrangements confuse him? I was about to find out. I moved his bed into my bedroom but didn't think he'd sleep in it. Instead of ushering him to the kitchen, I opened the living room door. But he trotted past it towards his cage because that's where he was used to going. It was difficult persuading him to follow me to my room. He wouldn't cross the threshold at first and lay on the carpet outside my room. I needed him close to me. The only way it would work was to chase him in. Closing the living room door, so he couldn't bolt back through, I got behind him, placed my hand on his bum and ushered him in. Once in, I closed the bedroom door. That was him, he couldn't go anywhere.

'I'm sorry Dobby,' I said, kneeling on the carpet.

His little face stared at me through his oversized cone, barely able to raise it in the air.

'You're better in here with Dad,' I whispered, a finger lifting the cone slightly so that my eyes could meet his. 'It's for your own good, pal,' I continued. 'It'll not be for much longer.'

Uncle Weh once bought me a Celtic blanket for my Christmas. This always lay folded at the foot of my bed. After a few days of Dobby getting used to my room at night, he nestled down on the Celtic blanket, or in between my legs. I've had restless leg syndrome for as long as I remember. Dobby couldn't get comfortable for his dad's legs jumping everywhere. Sometimes he did sleep in his own bed, but he didn't sleep much. All night, most nights, I heard him get out, turn around, and get in again. He repeated this several times during the night. If I lay in bed on my side before he had a chance to jump up beside me, he could then snuggle in behind my legs. This worked better for both of us.

~~~

Mum and I were confident, or at least hopeful that our next trip to the vet would be the last one. We'd been administering the medication as directed, and Mum and Dad didn't think his wound was as red.

'Dobbbyyyy,' Zoe called, as we entered the vet's.

'Aye, back again,' I replied, with a heavy sigh, Mum directing me to a seat next to the reception desk.

'Oh, he's so cute,' another receptionist said, putting the phone down, having just dealt with a client.

'I see you've still got your cone on, petal,' Zoe said, emerging from behind the desk.

'Aye, I'm hoping it can come off today,' I said, rolling my eyes.

'Yeah, we hope so, too.'

Dobby was starting to become wise to the fact he was going into the vet's and was unhappy about the frequent visits. However, once inside, trailing his oversized cone along the ground, he enjoyed cuddles and gently taking treats from a few eager hands.

The nurse carried Dobby through to the consultation room so the vet could examine him. I sat chewing on my fingernails for about ten minutes. My head dropped to my chest when I heard him trotting back, his cone battering off the walls.

'He's looking a lot better,' the nurse said when she returned, 'but we need to keep the cone on him for another week.'
~~~

'No luck,' Zoe said.

'I guess not,' I answered, with another heavy sigh.

'Well, it's for the best. I'm sure it'll be off when you come back next week,' she assured us.

'I hope so,' I said as we walked out with Dobby.

Zoe was right, and after three long, stressful weeks, the cone was ready to come off. We were so relieved when we heard the tiny pit patter of Dobby's paws trot along the corridor, without the sound of the cone crashing into the walls. I had my dog back. I could cuddle him again. I could feed him myself again. And I could play with him again. However, it was back to his cage at night. But as he lay sleeping in his cage, I lay awake. Dobby wasn't turning around in his bed all night beside me trying to get comfortable. I didn't hear tiny paws pad across the carpet to find somewhere else to lie down. And he wasn't jumping up to nestle his little body beside his dad's legs on the big bed.

Chapter 16

NINE MONTHS

We returned to training in early February. We had missed the first two sessions of Dobby's bronze classes, but he had achieved his foundation level training. Dad had allowed me to do more towards the end of his foundation training, but I mostly sat and observed. Training Dobby was one of my main goals. This wasn't going to happen if Dad continued to take charge. I was annoyed that Dad took over, but I knew I would do it alone one day.

The bronze award was a continuation of the foundation level, with additional changes. The bronze award aims to provide the handlers with a basic knowledge of understanding and training their dog. For the bronze test, dogs are not required to have completed the Puppy Foundation Assessment programme, so many of the exercises were similar. The scheme is designed to train your dog to be happy, contented, well behaved and under the control of their handler who understands their responsibility to the dog, their neighbours and to the community.

At the beginning of all sessions, Fiona walked around the hall greeting everyone and, most importantly, each dog by giving them a treat. At the same time, she carried out one of the tasks, which was to examine the dog as a vet would do. She checked the teeth and gums, throat and finished with the body and tail. Fiona also made sure the dog had the correct identification, and the owner carried poo bags. She made sure we were able to remove and attach the dog's collar and lead correctly. These three tasks were easy for me to undertake. Although I can't see, I could lift Dobby's lips and feel his teeth. And he allowed me to put his lead and collar on.

Dad and I encouraged Mum to attend some sessions, because, sooner or later, she might have to bring me if Dad couldn't. She loved Dobby, but she was still wary of dogs, having been bitten by them before. So Mum was reluctant but relented and joined us at times. I felt it important for me to re-familiarise myself with the hall, so I tried to sit in the same seat each week. I chose one in the corner beside the stage. This way, if I happened to lose my bearings, I could scan around for the stage and find my seat.

Fiona usually began with the *controlled walk* exercise—the same one Dad and I quarrelled over during Dobby's foundation level. I spoke to Dad prior to returning to training, insisting I do more this time. So, he walked with me around the hall. There was a slight difference with this exercise. There were turns involved. At Fiona's command, we had to turn in a different direction, and your dog had to move with you without pulling forward or backward. This was tricky, but Dad did not attempt to wrestle the lead from my belt. I handed Dad the lead if I was struggling, but I was determined to eventually do it alone.

A new element was introduced to the bronze level, which was to *control your dog at a door or gate*. I let Dad do this one. It didn't matter if it was Mum, Dad, or me, because we taught Dobby from an early age to wait. He has rarely gone out of the door or gate before us. Apart from this new, simpler task, most exercises were the same as the foundation level. Dad awaited Fiona's instructions, taking over again, statue like, Dobby's lead hanging limply in his hand. These were: *control on lead*; *sit*; *lie down*; and *stand!*' I could have performed those tasks on my own. He needed to hear those commands from me to know who his master was. The longer Dad took control, the more Dobby would answer to him, and not me. There was also the dreaded '*Return to handler!*' Although we worked on this at home, we didn't have other dogs to distract him. But the outcome was the same.

'You need something for him to focus on,' Fiona said, retrieving Dobby for another try.

'What d'you mean?'

'Has he got a favourite toy at home he loves to play with?'

'It's mainly balls he plays with now.'

'That'll do,' she encouraged. 'Anything to keep his focus on you.'

'There's a squeaky ball he plays with.'

'Bring that with you next time. And try and be a bit more vocal,' Fiona finished.

Although it was ten days after my birthday, we finally made it to the Royal for a drink. Because Dobby is my dog, it was important I took him out as much as I could. I always planned to walk Dobby on my own, something Dad said

I wouldn't manage to do. He said there would always be other people to take him out for me. We left my house and the four of us went to The Bank Bar for something to eat first, before heading to The Royal Hotel. Busy main roads were another area I wanted Dobby to get used to. Dad was careful, and too cautious. My belt was around my waist, and the lead attached to Dobby's collar. When we waited to cross the road, I tightened my hands around my crutch handles. My teeth locked together as I felt the lead lift in the air. Dad was holding the lead.

'What are you doing, Dad?' I yelled.

'I'm just helping.'

'No, you're not. You don't trust me with him.'

'I don't want him running onto the road if he sees something.'

I understood what Dad was trying to do. Dobby was only seven months old, and Dad was only thinking that he was doing well. He didn't want anything to happen to him, hence holding the lead. Mum and I walked Dobby most days, so she knew how he was with me. We had been walking him on Kilrenny Common, Johnny Doo's, the Dreel Meadows, and Dreelside park as well as on the main road.

Instead of the usual route to the park, we cut through the other side, alongside Mitchell Place, towards the main road. Once there, I shortened Dobby's lead so he was closer to me, gave him a treat and headed past the hairdressers' and along the front of Watson Place, which brought us back to the opening in front of my house—a route I had been familiar with when I had sight, but was harder now, especially with a dog. Dad was rarely out with me and walked Dobby *for* me. He wasn't aware of the progress we were making.

'He's right, Wullie,' Mum interjected, as we prepared to cross the road to The Bank. 'He's good with Billy.'

'Alright,' Dad said, letting the lead drop from his fingers.

'Sit, Dobby,' I instructed.

I often had to ask if he did sit, because I couldn't see if he plonked his bum down or not.

'Did he sit?' I asked.

'No,' Mum answered.

As long as he waited until I told him to cross the road, it didn't matter if he sat at the kerb or not.

Because I was with Mum and Dad, it was easier to sit at the table closest to the front door. The Royal was quiet for a Saturday night. In my experience, the pub started filling up around nine. And it was only about six. We weren't staying long. A couple of drinks and up the road. Dad always had a vodka and coke, and Mum had a wine or gin. Instead of my usual pint of Foster's, I drank a whisky with lemonade. I tend to do this when out with them because it takes longer to drink a pint.

A lot of locals knew I had a dog now. I'd been missing from the pubs at the weekends for months, and people began to ask where I was. There was a few aw's when people passed on the way to the toilets. The barmaid came round to give Dobby a treat.

'Sit nicely,' she said, lowering her palm.

'He will,' I said, as Dobby sat.

'He's very gentle,' she said, giving Dobby a stroke.

'Aye, he is,' I assured her, with Dobby by my side.

Dobby wasn't always by my side though, as Dad was still too protective, and held the lead firmly in his fist. Another man passed, who my dad knew from his days at school.

'What is it?' he asked.

'It's a dog,' I said, winding him up, as he'd done with me for many years.

'I know it's a dog,' he said, disgruntled. 'I meant, what breed is it?'

'He's a Jack Russell,' I said, a grin on my face.

We decided to head home but hadn't realised it had started to rain. It was coming down in sheets. To get Dobby up the road in a hurry, we handed Mum the lead. But he wouldn't go. He held back to wait for his dad and Grandad. Mum carried on herself, but we were soaked through, as our progress was slow. I let Dad take the lead, so we got home quicker. We were soaking by the time we made it, just in time for the Masked Singer. We enjoyed working out who was behind the mask.

~~~

There were a few days in the middle of February when the rain was torrential. Not the best time to ask my friend, Brian, to tidy the garden. Dobby had been digging too much, and I hoped that by laying new chips, he would stop. I tried to keep Dobby indoors while Brian got to work, so Dobby didn't see what he was up to. But I had to let him out for the toilet. Brian put new membrane down and fresh chips on top. He'd created a new, lovely garden by laying new chips. I liked the outcome, but so did Dobby. No sooner had Brian left than
~~~

Dobby was digging again. His paws worked at an amazing speed. His nose sniffed furiously like he had found vermin. He found the membrane, grabbed it tight in his teeth and hauled it apart, dragging it across the slabs. The chips were scattered everywhere. What a waste of time and money… In hindsight, I realised it was too early to make any changes to either the house or garden.

Later in February, I asked a question in one of my Facebook groups. I wanted to know if anyone could recommend a good upholsterer. Dobby had chewed a small hole at the bottom of the backrest of my couch. My suite was fifteen years old and needed replacing, but I had bought my suite with the money my Dae left me when he passed away. (Dae is a Local Fife dialect for Grandad.) I did say Jack Russells were intelligent, and Dobby was no different! He waited until I went for a cigarette before setting to work. The second he heard the click of the lighter, he started chewing the same bit, making the hole bigger. I received an answer from the group with a number for a local upholsterer. I phoned and he came the next day.

'There's not much I can do with this,' he said, investigating the damage. 'The best I can do is glue it, I'm afraid.'

'Really, that'll stop him from targeting the same bit,' I said, rolling my eyes.

'He'll not go near it when I put this stuff on,' he continued. 'He'll not like the smell of the glue.

'I'm not so sure.'

'It's either that or a completely new back, which will cost you. And it'll be a different colour.'

'Glue will be fine then.'

'My dog loves to play with empty plastic bottles,' he went on. 'He'll play for hours with them.'

'Not Dobby,' I said. 'He'll just destroy them. He chews the bottle until he gets the top off. And then he chews that until he gets the lid flat. He's terrible for anything plastic.'

'Really,' he said, attaching the two halves together.

'Aye, he's a nightmare for plastics. It's not just plastics, either. I caught him biting into an unopened can of juice. He pierced the can and lemonade squirted everywhere.'

'Is that right?' he said.

'Aye, it is. How much do I owe you?'

'Ah, it was just glue. Call it £20 to cover my petrol.'

I felt through my wallet for twenty, but I didn't have enough.

'I'm sorry, I only have fifteen,' I said, holding out the notes.

'That's fine.'

'Are you sure?'

'Aye, honestly.'

I thanked the man and showed him out. 'How long would the repair last?' I thought to myself, as I shuffled back through to the living room. I put it to the test by going for another cigarette, and the question was answered right away. I had just lit the thing when I heard teeth on leather. The only solution I could think of was to cover it up. So, I took the Celtic blanket from the end of my bed, rolled it up and placed it in front of the hole. I discovered later that he was probably doing it for attention and soon stopped.

Mum and Dad went away for a few days at the end of February. They could leave us and be happy knowing I would be fine on my own with Dobby. He was on two meals a day now, and I fed him on my own. Dobby was a fussy Jack Russell. And like his breeder suggested, I often had to put some ham or crush a treat through his food to encourage him. I wasn't fond of this, but if it helped him eat his meals, then so be it. Before leaving for a few days, they also made sure I had dog walkers in place, as I couldn't walk him by myself.

Mum and Dad began encouraging me to leave Dobby on his own more, which allowed me to get some exercise. Sometimes, if it was a nice day, Mum came up to dog-sit. She would indulge in a Danielle Steel or Josephine Cox novel, wearing her golf visor to shade the pages from the sun. But I learned that Dobby usually lay on the mat inside the door until his dad returned. I often walked down to the Bank or the Royal, had a coke or two before heading home. One day, when sipping my drink in the Royal, I spoke to the barman, Tam. I'd known him for years, as he had worked in a few pubs in the area, and we got on well. He was the same age as my dad, and Tam also used to play for me on my pool team. As I feared, despite the team doing well in my absence, players started to leave, including my friend Stuart. Some weren't keen on Big Al's management. A question was playing on my mind while I sat.

'Tam, are you doing anything this Wednesday?'

'No, why?' he replied, serving another punter.

'Mum and Dad are away for a few days, and I was wandering if you could help walk Dobby with me?'

Tam stayed in the same street, so asking him would be

ideal.

'No problem, Billy,' he said.

We arranged a suitable time around lunch time—when Mum and I usually walked Dobby.

It was Tuesday, the day before Tam agreed to assist me with Dobby when I had a burning thought! Dobby was good at walking with me and either Mum or Dad. And despite Dad saying, 'You'll never be able to walk Dobby on your own,' it couldn't be too difficult, could it? It was a beautiful end to one of the warmest Februarys on record. The sun was shining, and I decided Dobby would have his first walk on his own, with his dad. I fetched my belt and lead from the cupboard, and called to Dobby, who was sunning himself in the garden.

I held his collar in the air. He was hesitant because there was no Granny or Grandad. But he trotted towards me, presented his neck, and I clipped the lead on. After locking up, I opened the gate, asked him to wait, walked through the gate, and Dobby came out behind me. What Mum and Dad didn't know wouldn't hurt them. My legs trembled violently as we made our way towards the park. Dobby pulled slightly, but it was easier than I expected. He walked well. Up to a point, anyway. We managed to the park, along the cycle path, and back the usual route we take with Mum, when I sensed something wasn't right. Where had Dobby taken me? The paving stones under my feet felt different. Luckily, someone who knew me, stopped doing her gardening.

'Are you okay, Billy?' she asked.

'I think Dobby's taken me up the garden path,' I said, jerking my head in the direction of her voice.

'He has,' she replied. 'But not by much.' She chuckled, approaching us.

'It's my first time walking him on my own and I thought I could manage.'

'It's okay, you're just a little off course. Do you want me to help you home?'

'Back on course will be fine, thanks.'

She guided us in the right direction, and after a few turns, I knew where I was. My face tensed and turned a shade of pink. Despite telling her several times that I would be okay now, she assisted us all the way home. I thanked her before removing Dobby's lead. My first time wasn't a complete disaster but could have been better. Dobby would learn that wasn't the way he was supposed to go.

I was more confident when Tam arrived. I didn't tell him about the previous day. I treated it as if it was my first. Tam stood in the open doorway while I got ready. with the bright sunshine behind him, I could see that he was wearing a cap. I also wore one to keep the sun out of my eyes. We did the same route as the day before, but when I asked Tam to walk with Dobby and me around the park, he was puzzled when I turned left. I hadn't realised the council had put a cycle path down.

When I started going this way, I forgot this path used to be a gravel one. The other gravel path was too far for me. This time we managed with no mishaps, apart from one! I thought I'd brought everything with me but failed to bring the most important thing. Dobby stopped for a poop, and I hadn't picked up the poo bags. Instead of going home for them, Tam nipped to his house to find something to pick it up with. After all, he was only yards from his house. As we were nearing home, the woman from the previous day passed in her car, rolled down the window and said, 'You have help today.'

'Oh, aye, what was that about?' Tam asked.

I was busted. I explained to him what happened the previous day.

'So, you don't need me,' he said, his face in creases.

'No, I did,' I said. 'It was a lot safer with you,' I recovered.

The last few sessions of Dobby's bronze training were going well. I growled at times when Dad persisted in taking control. But I began to notice the effects when I took control. I had been taking a ball to class, as instructed, and it began to work. Before I called Dobby to me from the other end of the hall, he still looked from side-to-side to see which dog he would speak to first. The second Fiona released him, I squeaked the ball. He had second thoughts. I removed the ball from the inside of my sweatshirt pocket, held it in the air, squeaked it and called his name. He headed towards me instead. However, after stopping beside me, he then went to speak to other dogs. It was a work-in-progress, but I was confident we would crack it. Dobby did pass his bronze award.

~~~

We still took Dobby to places he enjoyed, and one day, in the middle of March, we chose Kilrenny Common. I threw the ball to him, and he brought it back. But on the next throw he left his ball un-fetched in the grass as he met a dog belonging
~~~

to an old school friend called Rebecca.

I became anxious in June 2019, because I hadn't found the dog I wanted. I'd been to the Royal and stumbled home late one Monday night. My thoughts turned to Rebecca. I messaged Jake, whom I thought was Rebecca's partner. He replied to me the next day, letting me know he'd passed my message onto Rebecca. I knew she had a dog and thought she might be helpful in choosing the right four-legged friend for me. She had a four-year-old cockapoo, called Koodgy, but his particular breed wouldn't suit me.

She wasn't able to come round on the Tuesday, but we made arrangements for her and Koodgy to visit me on the Wednesday. The bark at my front door announced they'd arrived, before Rebecca knocked. I hurried to the door and beckoned them in. Rebecca settled herself on the couch. She was the same, kind girl I knew from school. We spoke about our school days, but as good as my memory is, I couldn't remember much. Koodgy sat at my feet while we talked.

'So, what sort of dog are you interested in?

I explained to her the importance of a small dog, and the appropriate colour, while I stroked under Koodgy's ear. Although Koodgy was a beautiful cockapoo, she was black.

'I'm really after a Jack Russell,' I said.'

'Ah,' she replied, studying her phone. 'You know they need a lot of exercise.'

'Yeah, my dad said the same, but that's the sort of dog I'm looking for.'

'You get dogs similar to Jack Russells which don't need a lot of exercise,' she went on. 'Lhaso Lapsos don't need exercise.'

'A Lhaso what?' I asked, scratching my head.

'They're quite popular dogs,' she said.

She mentioned other dogs, such as a Maltese and a King Charles—all dogs she thought would be ideal for me.

Before she left, she dug her hand in her bag and drew out some dog treats.

'Hold out your hand,' she instructed.

I did and she dropped a few treats into my palm.

'Tell her to sit.'

I did, and she sat. She took the offered treats.

'You didn't give her them all, did you?'

'Yeah, was I not supposed to?'

'No, just a couple.'

'You didn't say how many, sorry.'

'That's okay,' she said with a chuckle.

Rebecca left me that evening with a lot to think about, but my mind was still set on a Jack Russell.

It was nine months since Rebecca and I had met to discuss dogs. And having heard we had met Jake and Koodgy at the common in March 2020, Rebecca came round to meet Dobby for the first time. She brought her son Ian along with Koodgy. Dobby and Koodgy pelted in and out of the back door playing with each other. He was so excited. I managed to get both dogs inside when I fetched some treats from the cupboard. I told both dogs to sit, and they did. I gave one treat to each dog, and handed the bag to Ian, so he could give them one, too. Rebecca was delighted Koodgy and Dobby got on well. She wasn't surprised I had decided on a Jack Russell, as she knew how stubborn I was at school.

<div style="text-align:center">~~~</div>

Dad started to be extremely busy with his fish round, so Mum took Dobby and me to start his silver award training. A virus was spreading across the world, and Dobby was almost nine months old. Dad had found an enclosed area for dogs to play. It was often quite busy, but Dad got us in the car and drove us the mile or so to check it out. It was like a large pen. It had an access gate at each end. There were no dogs in it that night. Dad filmed me as I threw a ball for Dobby and he brought it back. He dropped it at my feet almost every time. I often had to feel for it, but Dad picked it up if I couldn't find it. The pen was perfect to play with Dobby, but when Dad spotted someone with very large dogs entering from the other side, we called it a day. Dad had brought Dobby here before and didn't like the way some of the dogs behaved.

'I would like to come here more often, Dad.'

'Aye, well, we can do that,' he said as we made our way to the car.

But that night, the day Dobby was nine months old, was the last any of us were allowed to do anything together for a while.

Chapter 17

UNCAGED

YOU MUST STAY AT HOME was the message announced by Prime Minister, Boris Johnson on Monday 23rd March 2020. The announcement was expected, but I'd hoped it wouldn't happen. Throughout the last few weeks, people were gradually asked to stay at home. Huge numbers complied, but it wasn't enough.

It was estimated that coronavirus arose in October or November of 2019. Reports indicated that a first patient began to show symptoms as early as 1st December 2019; hence the name Covid-19. A number of cases were not discovered until later that month. Studies indicated that a few hundred people had been infected with the virus before the end of 2019. The virus was believed to have originated in Wuhan, China, but began quickly to spread worldwide. The first confirmed case of Covid-19 in the UK was detected on 31st January 2020 in York. And the first British person to die from Covid-19 was from Wales. In an attempt to curtail the spread of the virus, the government began restricting travel, especially if would-be travellers showed symptoms of fever, coughing and difficulty breathing.

Mum was a regular viewer of the news and noticed the spread of the virus in east Asian countries such as China and Hong Kong and expected a catastrophic outcome. I was aware of the rapid spread but didn't pay much attention until the number of cases increased in the UK.

I hoped if, and by the time the virus reached Britain, it would dissipate, but by early March, the British government slowly changed strategy from limited contact to putting tougher restrictions in place. It was reported that by 1st March the total number of cases in the UK had reached 36. By 12th March that had soared to 590. The government advised that anyone with a new continuous cough or fever should self-isolate for seven days.

The night before lockdown, and after we'd played with Dobby in the pen, I contacted Dobby's breeder. I had promised her I would send her regular photos and videos of him growing up, but I'd had second thoughts about that. Why should I? He was my dog. I could bring Dobby up on my own. When I got home, I opened WhatsApp, found the breeder's contact, and uploaded a few photos along with the video Dad had taken earlier that evening. I received a reply almost instantly.

'He has turned out lovely,' the message said.

'He's been well looked after, and I've trained him well. He's a loyal companion,' I replied.

'So sweet, thank you,' she said.

'I thought I'd send you a video and some pics, since he's nine months old today,' I said.

'He's lovely and thank you' was all I got.

<div align="center">~~~</div>

I phoned Dad on the morning of 23rd March. He was due to take me to look at new garden sheds. My one was so old and untreated—if Dobby didn't break bits off with his teeth, the next strong wind would blow it down.

'When are we leaving?' I asked.

'Everything's shut, Billy,' he replied.

'I know a lot of places are closed, Dad, but I thought the shed centre would still be open.'

'No, everything's closed,' he repeated.

Like everything else, my shed would have to wait.

Boris Johnson instructed everyone in the UK against non-essential travel and contact with others. He also advised people to avoid pubs, clubs and theatres and encouraged working from home. It was no surprise nothing was open. The Cheltenham Festival, which attracted 150,000 people, and a Champions League knock-out match in Liverpool were the last sporting events to be held before they too were brought to a halt.

The full impact really started to hit home when football matches were abandoned, which meant Dad and I couldn't go to watch our local team, East Fife. Dobby's dog training also stopped on 18th March, only two sessions into his silver award. More restrictions were put in place daily. Pregnant women, as well as people over seventy and people with certain health conditions were asked to self-isolate. This included Dad and me who both had health conditions. Schools closed on 20th March. Closure of pubs, restaurants, gyms, leisure centres, nightclubs, theatres and cinemas took effect on the same day.

I watched Boris Johnson's announcement that evening, and the message was clear. We were to stay at home.

It would have been easier before I got Dobby, but how was I supposed to stay at home now? Dobby and I were making progress. I was walking him on my own more—almost every day. Mum walked with us a lot but if she couldn't, she was happy to let us go ourselves. She often messaged telling us to start and she would catch up. I was getting fitter and stronger walking every day. Surely, I would still be able to walk my dog, and Mum would still be allowed to help.

Boris restricted everyone to one form of exercise a day, which I used to walk Dobby. But a walk with Mum or Dad was not allowed because they weren't part of the same household. However, to help a vulnerable person was permitted. If it meant saving thousands of lives, including my own, and my family's—of course I would comply. Although I didn't like it, I would stay away from Mum and Dad's house.

My helper wasn't able to support me with my university studies in person, so we moved over to WhatsApp. This way, we could continue by using video call. Although everyone's end-of-module assessment was cancelled, we all wanted to submit what would have been our final piece. Dad came to collect Dobby every morning, and instead of bringing him back, he kept him for a few hours, allowing me to do some university work. But not much work was done. My support worker and I had a laugh most days doing lockdown quizzes. I felt guilty about this. I didn't like it. It was pointless. Dobby could have been at home with me. Dad continued training Dobby each university morning. We continued this arrangement for the first four weeks of lockdown.

Despite me having to do more on my own, Dobby and I were coping well. Mum did visit the local supermarket to make sure I had plenty of things I could cook for myself as well as the essentials. Dad sometimes went instead but stopped going to prevent the risk of infection. I had a good supply of hand sanitiser and always kept a basin full of hot soapy water. Everybody was advised to wash their hands regularly, but I always made sure my hands were clean at all times. I encouraged Mum and Dad not to enter my house—or not too far, anyway.

The first Thursday night after lockdown had been announced, millions of us stood at our front doors at eight in the evening, clapping for keyworkers. A few minutes before eight, I fumbled with the catch and opened my living room window. I heard the neighbours preparing to clap the second I swung the window towards me. Dobby watched as I stood resting my knees against my coffee table for balance, wondering what was going on. When the church bell chimed, I started hearing clapping to the west, and down the street to the east. Whistling, and cheering bounced off the buildings. My living room window looked out onto the car park, and everyone who took part in the clap for keyworkers stood at their front door. So, the effect wasn't the same. I felt that I was the only one in the UK who clapped, looking across an empty car park. Ashamed, I hung my head, promising myself I would do things differently and stand at my front door the following Thursday.

It was the Saturday after the first clap for key workers. I had been putting Dobby in his cage for seven months and I felt that amount of time was sufficient. I remember kneeling in front of his cage when he was only a few months old when I smelled something sour. I was preparing to put Dobby in for the night when the odour filled my nostrils. It smelled like an old concrete toilet block that you used at an old football ground.

Before some football stadiums were modernised, they once had an open trough which ran along the floor. I found out why Dobby's cage had a sour smell. He had been reluctant to go outside to do the toilet. Instead of messing in his bed or on the runner tray, he had been peeing on a toy. Having discovered what he had been doing, I cleaned the cage thoroughly and encouraged him outside more often.

'Why does Dobby need a cage?' I remember asking his breeder before we picked him up.

'All my dogs are kept in a cage,' she responded. 'They are safe, and nothing can happen to them when you're out or go to bed.'

Although I was a dog owner for the first time, I only planned on Dobby's cage as temporary until he was toilet trained, and until he stopped chewing things in the house. I was aware a cage should be a safe environment for your dog and some people keep the cage so the dog can go in if it is stressed or overwhelmed. I used a cage because his breeder had advised me to, but once I was satisfied Dobby had been housetrained, the cage would go. I had never felt comfortable putting my dog in a cage.

Caged dogs made me think of the times I visited my friends in Shetland between 2006 and 2008. The first time was when Malky and Maxine invited me to stay. On this visit, Maxine and Jessica had three dogs between them now; one was a Saarloos wolf dog called Benji, one a collie-German shepherd cross called Goggles and the youngest, a beautiful black Staffordshire terrier called Barny. Goggles had been the dog I knew. Barny was only a small thing. They kept him in a cage. I felt uncomfortable listening to him rattling around in his enclosed space, like a boggart trying to break out of a cupboard, biting at his metal casing.

'Why do you keep Barny in that thing, Jessica?' I asked.

'Erm, he's a puppy. And a menace,' she replied. 'He needs to learn to behave, so I put him in when he's been bad.'

'He'll misbehave even more if you keep him in a cage,' I added, turning to the rattling sound.

Maxine and Jess's boyfriend remained quiet, as they didn't want to be part of our conversation. Jessica stared at me with a puzzled expression. Her mousy long hair hung limply by her round face.

'No,' she continued firmly. 'That's the way I feel best to teach him right from wrong.

'Yeah, I said. 'But d'you not feel there can be a better way to teach him what's right from wrong?'

'But...'

'I know he's your dog,' I interrupted.

'But he's my dog,' she tried to say again.

'Yes, I know. I'm just saying, it's not right using a cage as punishment.'

I was a guest for a week or so and I didn't want to upset my hosts, so I left it at that. I never wanted my dog trained in this way. My Shetland friends had been doing it wrong.

I was still preparing Dobby's bed for the night when I had second thoughts. Instead of putting Dobby in the cage, I slid the two bolts across, left the door open and walked away. He now had a choice. He could go in if he wanted or not. I still didn't allow him through to my bedroom while I sat in the living room. Instead of ushering him to his cage before I went to bed, I left the living room door open. He was unsure of what to do. I heard his little paws on the carpet, but he stopped short of my bedroom. Guide dogs are trained not to enter their owner's bedroom, but Dobby was not a guide dog. I wanted Dobby to sleep on the big bed beside his dad when I thought I was ready to let him. But Dad once said that the couch might be where he sleeps when he gets older. And after a few minutes, I heard him jump back onto the couch. I let out a long sigh, pulled the covers tight to my chin and rolled over. Some day he might jump up beside me.

~~~

'Oh, hi, Billy. I thought you would have been out for the Thursday clap last week,' my neighbour, Catherine, asked when she spotted me emerge from my front door.

'I was, but I opened my living room window instead,' I said, gripping the handrail for support.

'Well, we'll be out here every week.'

Almost everyone in our little corner stood at their front door. I knew about eighty per cent of the residents in my
~~~

street, some of them even before I moved in 2006. I began to see a lot more of them when I walked Dobby. I engaged in conversation with them and talked to a lot of new dogs and their owners—a lot of them who I didn't know.

The clock chimed and everyone began cheering for the NHS and keyworkers. Many clapped. Some shook objects, and others rattled tin cans. It was different from the previous week. I felt involved. I couldn't wait for the following Thursday. The only thing was, I was leaving Dobby on his own. He lay on the arm of the couch, his two front paws under his chin: his two back legs under him. He was the perfect width and length and lay snuggly as I left him for a few minutes.

Chapter 18

THE HOLY GRAIL

The streets were deserted. The skies empty of planes. There were few boats at sea. People were stranded abroad, or on cruise ships. Even the seagulls were quiet with no one around to feed them. It felt like a real-life *28 Weeks Later,* an infectious zombie movie which I like starring Robert Carlisle. A rage virus infects millions of people and spreads from their bites. 28 weeks later; the virus dissipates and there are a few survivors before the virus rages again.

It was unusually warm weather for early April, so I often left Dobby to wander in and out as he pleased. I used the opportunity to spend a lot of time with him and work on training as much as I could. There were still some things I was still struggling with—especially re-call. He was less destructive in the garden now, but if I heard him up to no good, I was hot on his case. He was a sun worshipper. He moved around the garden, finding a warm spot. If he was inside, he found a bright place on the couch to lie in. If it wasn't the weather for this, he pushed his dad's arm out of the way with his snout, and curled up beside me, my arm under his body while I watched the telly.

163

Dad had put Dobby's cage in the shed along with the rest of the junk. Dobby wasn't using it anymore, so what was the point in it taking up floor space. My kitchen was almost back to its original state. In place of the cage were bags of kibble, which were lined against the wall, with his water bowl in front. I gave Dobby a variety of dry food, so he didn't get fed up with the same every day.

But he was still a fussy eater. He liked the duck and rice for a while. He ate the salmon and rice for a while. He nibbled the turkey and rice for a while. But he was never keen on the lamb and rice. It didn't matter what I put down to him, because he often turned his nose up at it. Some people said that it can take a long time before you find the right brand and combination which your dog will enjoy. One day I would crack it. He was, however, down to two meals a day, which meant I didn't have to get up as early. And I set the radio station, Forth One, to wake me at seven instead of six.

The next clap for keyworkers came around, and because Dobby was toilet trained and his cage was gone, I was happy to leave him to wander about the house. Except my bedroom. He wasn't ready to be left in there unattended. It was still important, pandemic or not, to leave Dobby on his own for periods of time. With Dobby settled on the arm of the couch, I made my way to the front door. The same residents were standing waiting with their tin cans and other rattley objects. Anne approached me with something to shake. It was a simple coke bottle filled with stones. This time I could properly join in. But something else happened. Just as the church bell chimed eight, music began to play. A neighbour brought out a Bluetooth speaker and played *Simply the Best,* by Tina Turner. I believe it was to keep everyone's spirits raised.

Some sang along, except for me, as I am a Celtic fan and *Simply The Best* is associated with Rangers supporters. Some clapped. Some shook their objects along to the music. And some tried a combination of all three. This performance was recorded and uploaded to social media. When I returned to Dobby, he was still on the arm of the couch where I had left him. I didn't expect any different, as he'd calmed down a lot and he'd stopped chewing the hole at the bottom of the backrest of the couch. The lockdown routines continued each Thursday for the next six weeks.

My telly was on almost every day after Boris Johnson announced lockdown. I mostly watched news channels such as BBC News and Sky News as well as the Andrew Marr show on a Sunday morning. I was struck by the events happening in northeast Italy. It was frightening. If thousands of people were dying in Italy and Spain, we couldn't be far behind. The government monitored the spread and worked out we were three weeks behind Western European countries. I hoped, watching these channels, promising updates would arrive. If I wasn't watching the news channels, I made sure I tuned in for Nicola Sturgeon's daily briefing. Not only was I keen to hear of developments, but I was also hoping the virus had slowed so we could celebrate Dobby's first birthday, which was fast approaching.

I never felt confident walking Dobby in new areas or places I hadn't been to for a while, because of the amount of eyesight I'd lost. One such area was the far side of the park where the gravel path led. I only walked this route with Mum. The path was simple enough, but someone with little sight could easily wander off track.

I remember an area with a few bushes, and it reminded me of when a few friends and I played up the park. They'd just finished primary school, and I'd just finished second year at high school. Truth or dare was a favourite pastime. My cousin dared me and another girl to kiss. She was a nice-looking girl with long blonde hair and beautiful blue eyes. She liked me on and off throughout primary school, and me her. So, it wasn't so much as a dare for us, but a pleasure. She was too shy to do the deed in front of everyone, so we disappeared behind the bushes. Despite the warm evening, her lips were soft and ice cold, like she'd just sucked on a strawberry ice lolly. It was so romantic under the fading night sky. We returned smiling from ear to ear. The pleasure was short-lived. My cousin asked how it went, and I told her, 'It was okay I suppose.' My cousin often treated her badly, and she deliberately wanted to embarrass the girl and wanted me to treat the kiss as a joke. The girl was like *Little Red Riding Hood* in her white shorts and red T-shirt running from the big bad wolf, as she ran all the way home—her hair flowing behind her. She disappeared out of sight like a bat in the night sky, swooping to pluck a fly from the air as it took flight. I wished my cousin hadn't set us up. The kiss meant something. We both wanted it. But my cousin had to spoil it. *I* felt like the wolf.

Mum, Dobby and I reached the bushes. I found the girl online many years later, added her as a friend on Facebook and apologised for what happened. She said she couldn't remember being set up, but I thought she didn't want to re-visit that night she was made fool of by my cousin and me.

<div style="text-align:center">~~~</div>

Towards the end of April, and after four weeks of isolation, Dad returned to work. But he didn't expect so much demand for fish. He was over-the-head with customers—many of them new ones. Because everything had closed down, there were more people at home, and some of them didn't realise a fish van came up their street. More people wanted fish. Dad struggled to cope with the demand. He needed help. And the help came in the form of Mum.

She and Dad had had a van each at one stage and shared the round between them. She knew how to be a fish merchant and now was needed to be one again. Mum and Dad purchased another van, my brother, a skilled joiner, kitted it out in super-quick time, and the vehicle was ready to go by the beginning of May. This meant that Mum and Dad were late home most nights. One of them managed either to walk Dobby in the morning or night but were starting to struggle to fulfil walking duties. It meant that they missed the clap for key workers. Because they were so busy, they suggested I would be better organising a dog walker for a Tuesday and Thursday.

I had no idea who to contact to arrange a dog walker, so I tried my doctor's surgery in the first instance. The receptionist provided me with a Fife Council emergency crisis number, which I phoned. I provided the receptionist with some details of why I was requiring help, and she told me someone would be in touch. I heard my mobile ring while I took a shower and couldn't possibly get to it in time.

I received a text message explaining she was contacting me from the East Neuk Community Emergency Planning Team and had been able to arrange a dog walker for me. I messaged her back apologising for missing her call and that I would be around to answer the phone if she called back, which she did. She let me know about the volunteer dog walker she'd managed to find. He was called Ellis. Ellis and his wife lived across the road. They knew me, but I didn't think I knew Ellis. But I remember meeting him on the bus home one night. The bus was at a standstill because someone had fallen into the middle of the road. Some passengers, including Ellis, decided they would be quicker walking. We made the appropriate arrangements, and Ellis was in place for Tuesdays and Thursdays.

With nothing to do most nights, I often watched the telly, whether it be quiz programmes, a movie, or re-runs of football matches. I wasn't fussed for alcohol; it didn't bother me. Saturday nights were different! I had got into the habit of drinking prosecco when my university support worker started working for me in 2012. He and his wife often came round for prosecco day sessions. I never drank prosecco when I frequented the pubs before I got Dobby. I was in most weekends now, so had a bottle or two most Saturday nights while Dobby curled up beside me or lay in his bed. He sometimes preferred the top of the backrest behind me. His little head drooped over the side close to my shoulder. I glanced to my left, spotting two lines of long-lashed eyelids closed.

I had a particular wine glass I favoured. It didn't have a circular base like other wine glasses. This one had a thicker stem, which widened from bottom to top, like a miniature vase. Unfortunately, this glass broke, and I was unable to find another like it. There were more wine glasses in the cupboard. But nothing compared to the original one I had. Mum searched thoroughly for another one but was unsuccessful. She did, however, find a suitable replacement. It has a thick base and stem, which widens out like a small bowl. It can also be used for gin. And it can hold half a bottle of prosecco, meaning fewer visits to refill it.

'*Indiana Jones and the Last Crusade,*' is my favourite *Indiana Jones* movie—a film in which a group of archaeologists go in search of the Holy Grail. It is believed if you drink from the cup of Christ, it will give you the gift of eternal life. However, in the movie, if you don't choose wisely, the wrong cup can have devastating consequences. Obviously, Indiana chose wisely. My wine glass has a close resemblance to The Holy Grail.

While I sat each Saturday night with The Holy Grail, I would video-call friends I hadn't spoken to for a long time. Some were happy to talk, and those who didn't answer, obviously weren't. Because Dobby is such a quiet dog, it's always been difficult to know if he is awake or sleeping. The first time I heard him dreaming was when he was a few months old. He began to whimper in his sleep. This is when I know he is sleeping. But I can be caught off guard when I'm holding the Holy Grail in my hand and Dobby suddenly starts to dream. It startled me and the prosecco left my glass and covered both Dobby and me.

<div align="center">~~~</div>

A Facebook group member enquired if anyone had a dog cage they no longer needed. It was a site where people gave away or collected unwanted items for free. Dobby's cage was in my shed, so I was happy to pass it on. It was better going to someone who would get the use of it. Besides, Dad had arranged for someone to knock my shed down and take it away, along with everything in it—apart from my wheelchair. That had to be kept in my front cupboard until I got a new shed.

It took only one smack of the hammer and the whole thing collapsed. I was glad to get rid of the thing. But having no shed created additional problems. It gave Dobby a bigger area to explore, but not having mastered recall, it was harder to locate him. I really had to work harder at the blasted recall.

Chapter 19

LIVING THE HIGH LIFE

Dobby was nearly twelve months old, and it's amazing how dogs learn to adapt to different paces. He walked quicker with Dad. He was slightly slower with Mum, and he completely slowed down when he walked with me. Was this because he adapted to my disability? He pulled to begin with, but the more we trained him to stop pulling, the more he did it. A simple 'wait' or 'don't pull,' was enough. I remembered Fiona's instruction to keep your dog focused on you. She said to talk to your dog about anything, so I spoke about what was on the telly. Sometimes I had to give the lead a tug if he began sniffing at something. Despite people saying I wouldn't manage to walk Dobby he loved his walks with his dad.

A lot of people had their doubts about me owning a dog. One concern was how I would pick up my dog's poop. I remember when I got home from viewing Luna in August 2019 and went straight to the pub. A man had said, 'What are you going to do with a dog?' I'd forgotten my wallet and Dad came back with it to see the man's arms flailing like King Louie from *The Jungle Book*.

'What was that guy's problem?' Dad asked me the following day.

'Ah, he was telling me I wouldn't manage a dog.'

No one taught Dobby to do his business in the garden before his walks. Another of my conditions of owning a dog had failed. So, I had to pick it up. Guide dog owners were exempt from picking up after their dog—although the advice from the Guide Dogs society is that if you are registered with a sight impairment or not, they should try. I wondered if it was the same for people who were registered blind and owned a pet dog, so I called them to find out. Unfortunately, it applied only to people with guide dogs. However, if Dobby pooped on his walk, I wouldn't deliberately leave it. It's not in my nature. Dobby did, now and again, stop to do his business. If I think he did anything, I pulled a bag from the holder, knelt on the ground, put my hand in the bag and swept for it. Like in Dobby's Garden, he never did a poop on the path. He dropped it on the stones, or grass verge. But I learned to know if he had done it on our walks. If the retractable lead tightened and Dobby wouldn't budge, it was a sign he needed to go. I watched his back end closely and if he jumped out of the way, he had done something. I followed where his bum had been. This was easier to find because I smelled it.

I hadn't realised that when other people were out with Dobby, they were letting him walk off the lead. Of course, he had plenty of runs along the beach with his granny, grandad, or Uncle Weh. Beaches were something I had to accept I wouldn't manage. I didn't think Dobby was ready to walk off the lead. He wasn't biddable enough yet. He still didn't return when he was called. Some day I planned to walk

Dobby off the lead, but this was another thing Dad said I wouldn't manage to do.

~~~

Approaching the end of May, I was hopeful Dobby's party would go ahead. In preparation, I set things in motion. Because Dad was a good bricklayer, I wanted places for my guests to sit, so I asked Dad to build a small L-shaped wall at the bottom of the garden. He did this most weekends when he wasn't working, and it began to take shape. I ordered a gazebo and a turntable optic stand from Amazon. I wanted to plan if restrictions allowed more people to mix.

We'd still been performing our *Dreelside Shenanigans* routines each Thursday. The *Dreelside Shenanigans* had been a name our small corner of neighbours had made up. We rehearsed and recorded the performances in the afternoon. We took several attempts to get the routines right which meant, as well as leaving Dobby in the house on his own for a few minutes at night, he was also being left for an hour or so during the afternoon. We uploaded the recordings to Facebook in the evening, after the clap for keyworkers. Some-times I stayed out for longer to have some prosecco with my neighbours—again leaving Dobby on his own for a while.

I was aware of other people performing various socially distanced street parties and routines. This was our way of coming together during these scary times. It was good to take part in something fun and took your mind off the pandemic for a while. The community coming together during these difficult times was a reminder of how close family and friends
~~~

were. One week we made up a routine to *500 Miles,* by The Proclaimers. And later that evening a local man performed a mixed acoustic version of Bob Marley songs. Chris, with his hippy look—shorts and T-shirt, long dark hair tied in a bun, belted out the notes.

When I went back inside to Dobby, he wasn't where I usually leave him. I had been neglecting him too much to join my neighbours every week. To make sure he didn't pinch anything from the kitchen table while I was out, I tucked one chair under and left the other out a fair distance. I left him in the usual place on the couch, but I forgot to position the kitchen chairs. Items were knocked from the table. Things were scattered everywhere. Empty bottles rolled across the floor. Stuffing was sticking out from the arm of the couch. There was no point in telling him off. It was my fault for leaving him for longer each week. He needed to take his frustration out on something, so when his dad was away, Dobby played.

After Chris's live performance, I decided to do a couple of my own. The following week, after we'd performed a routine to *YMCA* by The Village People, I dug out my Johnny Cash wig, found my cowboy hat and did a version of *Ring of Fire.* I safely left Dobby in the kitchen with both chairs positioned correctly this time. I used my Bluetooth speaker with my backing track on my iPhone. I was used to singing Johnny Cash songs on the karaoke most weekends in the pub but hadn't sung since 2018. There were further performances by the *Dreelside Shenanigans* but, a few days before the end of May, the country was asked to bring the weekly clap for keyworkers to a close. This meant an end to the *Dreelside Shenanigans*. but not before a last performance by me.

Dominic Cummings was big in the news, having driven home from London to Durham and then to the town of Barnard Castle. He claimed he was testing his eyesight despite knowing he was positive with Covid.

We performed a routine to *We're all Going on a Summer Holiday* but changed the word '*all*' to '*not*' and added 'but Dominic Cummings is' at the end. The *Dreelside Shenanigans* and I got the ladies together and I performed a mash-up of *Lucille*, by Kenny Rogers and *All the Single Ladies*, by Beyonce—changing the lyrics to *All the Dreelside Ladies*.

~~~

The Scottish government was still taking a cautious approach to Covid-19 by the middle of June. Although the virus was now in a downward trend, over 2000 people in Scotland had lost their lives since statistics were recorded from the 5th of March. There were fewer people in hospital. Fewer deaths were recorded, and more people were being discharged from hospital. However, at this stage of lockdown, large groups of people were still not permitted to gather.

My hopes of holding a party for Dobby's first birthday were diminishing and I had to concede that Dobby's party couldn't go ahead. Dad had completed the wall in time for the party, but it would still be there for when we would be permitted to have larger gatherings. My neighbour, Lynne, who took part in the *Dreelside Shenanigans* suggested I plan a party for Gotcha Day, the day I got Dobby home. If restrictions
~~~

allowed, I would have it in September instead.

It was around the same time in June when Dad took Dobby away for a while. It wasn't until he brought Dobby back that he told me where he'd taken him. A small number of my family decided that, despite restrictions, they would have a picnic at the top of Billow Ness. Dad knew I wouldn't want to take the risk, so he didn't tell me. I would have liked the opportunity to make up my own mind. At least Dobby was away from the house for a bit, allowing me some time on my own.

He was often away from the house during the summer of lockdown. Sometimes for too long. Uncle Weh and my nephew, Mikey, took him up the park for a run and they lost balls in the long grass because Dobby didn't go after them. Mum and Dad took him to St Andrews for a run along the West Sands beach. I constantly pushed the button on my talking watch. How long had he been away? Had something happened to him? Was he ever coming home? These thoughts ran around my head every time he was gone a while. When they returned Dobby from the Billow Ness picnic, I learned he'd scaled Johnny Doo's Pulpit Rock. 'Clever boy, Dobby,' I said, stroking him under his chin, when Dad had brought him back. I knew, one day, because I couldn't, he would climb My Rock.

A few days before Dobby's birthday, my mobile rang. I didn't recognise the number, but I took the call. It was difficult balancing everything. Taking from Dobby whatever he had in his mouth. Holding the phone whilst opening the outside bucket lid. And trying to keep my own balance.

'Is this William?' a woman's voice asked.

'Yes, this is he,' I answered.

I rarely went by my birth name, so I corrected her.

'I prefer Billy.'

'My name is Margaret, and I'm calling from the RNIB. Have you heard of us?'

Of course, I had. I'd used them since I was registered blind in 2000.

'Yes, I have,' I said, still balancing the phone while I made my way inside to sit down. 'But I only use the RNIB when I need them,' I went on.

'Are you aware of the services we provide?'

'Not really.'

She explained the wide range of services they offered on Teams, including many community groups, such as a film group. a community quiz; a campaigns call; and a football call. She explained about many more, and I was glad I had answered my mobile.

'Oh, right,' I said, paying more attention.

'Would this be something you would be interested in?'

'Yes, I think I will be.'

'Are there any of these groups you would like to join?'

'I would be interested in a few of the ones you have mentioned. Particularly the quiz, film group and football call.'

'That's great,' she replied. 'I'm the Community Connection Co-ordinator for your area so I'll send you information regarding the various joining details. What format do you prefer?'

'E-mail is my preferred format,' I told her.

'Okay, great. I'll send you over the information you need and let the team leaders know you will be joining their groups.'

I had something else to look forward to now, rather than falling asleep while watching the news. I was, however, apprehensive about joining these groups and talking to new people for the first time. But it might be a good thing interacting and talking to people in the same situation as myself, which I hadn't done for a few years. The last time I'd been involved in anything like this was in 2011, when I attended an eleven-day positive steps programme in Edinburgh.

The Community Connection Co-ordinator who ran the quiz on a Friday evening gave us good news, but false hope. She said we might be able to get out soon, as the virus seemed to be slowing down. There were around twenty people who participated in the quiz, and I quickly began interacting with a few of them. I was an instant success having watched quiz programmes most of my life. It turned out a lot of people who took part in the quiz also took part in the other groups such as the film group and football call. Before I knew it, I was accepting friend requests on Facebook. The co-ordinator for the football call contacted me via messenger to ask about the teams I followed. He was surprised when I mentioned East Fife. But when I let him know that I also followed Celtic and Arsenal, he said there were a couple of Celtic fans, along with Rangers, Hibernian and Hearts fans and that I should fit in nicely.

Because the football call was held midday on a Saturday, I often had a lie down on the settee while I talked on my mobile. But I didn't do much talking… I didn't get a chance. The people were so enthusiastic speaking about their own teams, I barely got a word in. Dobby often lay in between my legs, or under my arm, beside me on the couch. Someone said, if your dog lies across your lap, it's a sign of loyalty. I quickly became friends with Lewis, Jan, Claire and Carl—who preferred to be called Macar, referring to the fact he was a Sunderland supporter, although he also followed Hibernian, and Scotland.

By the end of June, restrictions did indeed begin to ease, allowing more people to mix. However, this was too late to celebrate Dobby's birthday, which was a quiet one spent in the garden with his dad, granny and grandad. He wasn't spoiled as much as we wanted, but he got a few presents—mostly indestructible toys, along with a few treats.

Dobby still didn't eat much, which was a concern, so I decided to change his food. The person who had told me that it could take years to find the right blend for your dog was right. Dobby hasn't had the greatest stomach since he was little. There was a time when his poop was solid, but didn't last long, as he got fed up with the same, particular food at that time. I don't think I helped by trying him with different kibble. I didn't realise you had to gradually switch over from one brand to another. Dobby had to eat so I tried one of the online retailers who tailor the food for the type of dog you have. I had to try something because I was fed up with him not eating his food.

~~~
~~~

Almost four months had passed since I set foot in Mum and Dad's. They often said there was no Covid in their house. Mum kept a clean and tidy house but how did they know there were no traces? However, it was a relief to be back at Mum and Dad's. I managed on my own, but I relied on things which were easy to cook and sometimes I ordered a takeaway meal. A takeaway meal is what we had: fish and chips from Anstruther's golf club restaurant.

Afterwards, Dad walked Dobby and me up the road. A meeting was organised with the *Dreelside Shenanigans* to see if we wanted to continue with the lockdown routines. I tried walking Dobby through the house on his lead, but he wouldn't go so we took the long route around to the front. No one wanted to continue, so it really was the end of the *Dreelside Shenanigans*. But it meant that I could spend more time with Dobby.

I continued to leave doors open in the off-chance Dobby would come gradually through to my bedroom at night. He still wasn't sure and slept on the couch or the top of the backrest. But he tried his luck at times. Gradually he edged closer into the room, and before long, he jumped onto the big bed beside his dad. The corners of my lips rose as he settled beside his dad. He preferred living the high life. I made sure I positioned myself so he could snuggle his little body into the groove of my legs. As long as Dobby was happy, then so was I.

Chapter 20

CAPTAIN DOBBY

Most of the early part of May 2020 had been spent creating a playlist for a birthday party that didn't happen. I used my Alexa device and called it *Dobby's Birthday Playlist.* Using the Google function on my iPhone, I found the first *Now, That's What I Call Music* album which was released in 1983—the year after I was born. I had plenty of songs to pick from. Dobby was either sunning himself in the garden or lying beside me on the couch. He might have thought it strange every time I called out, 'Alexa, play… and, add this song to *Dobby's Birthday Playlist.*' It took over a month to sift through every *Now, That's What I Call Music* album but once I'd reached the latest one, the playlist was complete.

Then, Dobby's new food arrived in a big cardboard box, but instead of waiting for Mum or Dad to help, I broke open the box. I was impatient and wanted to see what I'd bought. However, when Mum and Dad came over later that day, Dad took it outside to examine what was inside. I sat on the newly built wall while Mum boiled the kettle. He talked me through the contents. It contained a huge bag of dry, oversized kibble, which was too big for Dobby's mouth. It also had trays of pre-cooked wet food, along with multiple bags of chew sticks.

'You'll have to gradually change Dobby over from the old dry food to the new one,' Dad explained.

I'd raised Dobby for nearly a year, and I think I knew how to switch Dobby's food over without having to be told how to.

'Yeah, I realise that, Dad.'

'Oh, it has a wee chart on how to switch over,' he continued.

'That's good,' I said.

'I'm not sure about this wet food,' he said, turning his attention to the trays.

'What d'you mean?'

'There's not much substance to this wet food and it's full of vegetables. I'm not sure how you'll manage to portion this stuff up.'

Mum had been listening to us through the open kitchen window.

'Wullie, we'll portion it up for Billy,' she said, coming outside to join us, carrying two cups of tea.

Allowing Mum and Dad to do this made me less independent because I was used to preparing Dobby's food on my own. But Dad was right. The only good thing about wet food was I didn't have to gradually switch him from Pedigree Chum.

Dobby managed to break the bigger chunks of kibble into smaller, manageable bitesize pieces. His wet food was gone in seconds. Mum or Dad quartered the wet food. This made it easier for me and I'd finally found a combination that worked.

Restrictions began to ease, and people were allowed to meet up more, as long as it was outside. This meant you could go to the pub, but only if they had a beer garden. Mingling inside was still not permitted.

I had lost a lot of weight since getting Dobby because I wasn't drinking pints five nights each week. And I was walking Dobby every day. I still had my Holy Grail in the house on a Saturday night and ordered the odd delivery from The Anstruther Boat House or Chinese takeaway. Apart from that, I wasn't missing a drink. However, because you could go to the pub again, it seemed rude not to.

I fetched Dobby's retractable lead from the cupboard, threaded the handle through my belt and dangled his collar. He made his way inside, lay down and presented his neck as normal. Once ready, we set off. A mid-afternoon pint wasn't my style, but a cool lager in the glorious sunshine sounded refreshing. Dobby and I hadn't walked this way on our own before. In fact, it was the first time I'd walked him to the pub. Dobby seemed to know where we were headed. He walked happily on my left-hand side. Fiona had taught us the crossover technique. Your dog walked on the inside away from the road and Guide Dogs train a dog to walk on your left. When I told him to wait before crossing the road, he did. I always carried a treat pouch with me.

'Good boy,' I said, lowering my hand to give him his reward.

We reached the Royal, and we walked to the back entrance. I wasn't used to this way. The pool team often left via the back door if we had an away match and someone took a car, but

I had never done it alone. I couldn't find my way in. When I get myself lost, I normally try to retrace my steps, listening for the traffic and voices. Dobby was no help, so I called the pub. Tam answered and after telling him I needed help, he came and rescued us.

'Why didn't you use the front door?' Tam said, opening the gate.

'I didn't think you were allowed in the pub,' I replied, following the sound of Tam's voice.

'You can walk through the pub to get to the beer garden as long as you wear a mask,' he said, as I approached him.

'I'll know that in future,' I said, manoeuvring Dobby through the gate.

Tam made sure I found myself a seat before going to get me a pint. The place hadn't changed. I'd been in the beer garden a few times but used the back door to get there. The same people whom I'd known for years had mingled inside the pub but now sat outside. I tried to identify the voices belonging to each person. It wasn't too difficult. Because a lot of these people were late morning or afternoon drinkers, it was the first time they'd met Dobby. Once I was settled with my pint, I let Dobby off the lead so he could wander about. A woman was concerned in case he ran out of the gate. But Dobby wouldn't run away. The gate of my back garden was often open while I sat in the sunshine, and I didn't realise it had been open. The two boys across the road often teased Dobby by poking a stick through the fence.

'You'll not get that back if Dobby gets a hold of it,' I told one of the boys. I think they often flicked the gate latch and left it open. The only reason I knew it was open was when the woman from the chemist delivered my medication.

I said to Helen in the beer garden, 'It's okay; he won't leave.'

'He's got his nose under the gate,' she said.

'He's just curious,' I continued. 'If you keep an eye on him anyway, just in case, that'll be great.'

'He's such a lovely wee thing,' she said, as she sat admiring him from the table to my right.

As I had predicted, Dobby didn't go under the gate. He went to speak to other people sitting outside. He came back to me when the manageress appeared with dog biscuits. I gave him a couple, because I was worried about his stomach. I only had two pints, and even though I enjoyed chatting to regulars, I didn't want to stay long so I called Dobby to me and re-attached his lead and walked up the road.

Although he was enjoying his food, we experienced another problem. Dobby's wet food went straight through him. The experiment didn't work. Would I ever get it right? I had to stop to pick Dobby's poop up when I walked him home from the pub. But pick what up? It was all diarrhoea. My hands were covered in the stuff. I retched at the smell of my poop covered hands as I attempted to bag it up, gathering more stones than poop. I had to make do and wash my hands, and crutch handles when I got home. Careful not to smother the door handle, I used my little finger to push the handle down. After filling the basin with soapy water, I thoroughly washed my hands and scrubbed my crutch handles.

'You shouldn't have taken Dobby to the pub when his poops are like that,' Dad said, when he heard we'd snuck out.

'I know, Dad. I thought he was alright.'

Dobby's stool was far too loose with the new food. His dry kibble was counteracting his wet food to a certain extent, but I had to put him back to what he was on before. I could have kept Dobby on the dry food, but crossed him over to his old kibble, too. Once Dobby was completely changed back to his original food, I decided to contact his breeder again.

It took me a long time to find her number on WhatsApp because I'd had no contact with her since March. She told Dad and me when we collected Dobby that he would never have diarrhoea if he ate his biscuits. I'd been hunting high and low on Pets at Home, Amazon and other pet stores for biscuits. I hadn't a clue what I was looking for and I still couldn't find the bloody biscuits. And because Dobby had diarrhoea so often, I thought it would be best to give her a phone.

I explained to her that I was introducing Dobby to adult food and asked for recommendations of which biscuits to put Dobby on. She said to give him whatever I liked within his age range.

'I've been giving him bone biscuits every day,' I told her.

'What?' she yelled down the phone.

'I have been giving Dobby his wet food, with a cup of dry pellets,' I said. 'And because you insisted, I give him biscuits, I've been putting little bone biscuits in his bowl.'

'His dry food is his biscuits,' she said, raising her voice. 'I hope you've been giving him his daily amount of kibble.'

'Of course, I have, I'm not that stupid. If you explained everything to me when we collected Dobby, instead of explaining everything to Dad, I wouldn't be having this conversation,' I bellowed.

'Every dog owner knows kibble are biscuits.'

'Well, I'm a dog owner for the first time, and I didn't!'

'I thought you knew,' she insisted.

'No, I didn't' I said, hanging up on her, crushing my hands into fists.

Dobby was a healthy dog, but I had to concede that he had a sensitive stomach. It was still a constant concern. I had to keep an eye on what he ate. This meant watching which treats to give him, as certain brands didn't agree with him. And he was back to his previous food. I waited until Dobby no longer had diarrhoea before taking him anywhere.

~~~

Mum and Dad owned a 22-foot sailing yacht, which sat in Anstruther harbour. They had bought it from my uncle in the late 2000s. Dad spent thirty-five years as a fisherman and fourteen years as a fish merchant. He considered a creel boat but got a yacht instead because he also secured a berth on one of the pontoons. Mum and Dad called it Myakey, a combination of my niece and nephews names, Mya and Mikey.

During the 1990s the first yachts began appearing in Anstruther harbour, alongside a few motorboats, speedboats and luxury pleasure cruisers moored to the middle and west piers. Throughout the decade, these boats multiplied as the number of fishing trawlers continued to drop. In the late 1990s, the local council approved plans to construct floating pontoons in the harbour. I remember listening to the dredger whirring day and night and I heard the crane swivel and pivot
~~~

as work began constructing the pontoons.

One night, as I peered across the water, I heard bells clanging and chiming in the wind. It sounded like the start of the movie *Jaws* when the woman took a midnight swim and had to grab the buoy when the shark attacked. Phase one was completed in 2000 and accommodated thirty-two boats. The pontoons rise and fall with the tide. When the tide is out, the gangway tilts to a 45-degree angle. The council introduced a second phase, which opened in July 2005, accommodating up to one hundred boats. Myakey was moored to the first erected pontoon. Perimeter fences like those from *Jurassic Park* were erected around the pontoons and you could only gain access if you have a fob.

I had been sailing many times on Myakey with Mum and Dad and sometimes on my own with Dad. But it was always safer with Mum to help. I remember when Dad and I went out on our own one day. It was nearing the end of the sailing season, and we knew that the next weekend the giant crane would rumble down the pier to lift the boats out of the water for the winter. However, there is always time for one last trip and the weather in October has been good for sailing in recent years.

The dodgers were an issue for me in getting on board the yacht. A dodger, also known as a spray hood, is an enclosed structure that protects you and the cockpit from wind, waves and weather. They could also be used to feature a frame-supported canvas on the top, sides and front. The boat's name is displayed on the dodger. Most people lift their leg over it and step onto the boat, but because I couldn't, Dad unclipped it so he could get me onto the boat. I sat on the side and Dad lifted my legs and swung them over the lifeline, careful not to tip me into the water. Then he began the process of countless checks he needed to perform before he untied the mooring ropes and hauled in the fenders.

The engine or outboard motor has to be used to navigate away from the pontoon and out of the harbour. According to Dad, you should never sail your way out of or into the harbour as the engine gives more control and manoeuvrability. The motor is switched to idling and when we get 100 yards offshore, the sails can be put up.

'It's a wee bit windier than I thought it was going to be, Billy,' Dad said, a safe distance from the creels. 'I'll need you to work the tiller while I go and raise the halyard. We'll not go anywhere if the main sail's not up.'

'Aye okay, Dad, no problem,' I said, as if I had a clue what he was talking about. 'What do I do with the thing?' I yelled, as he guided my hand onto the wooden rod.

No matter how many times I've been out in *Myakey* with Dad I never got the hang of sailing. Never mind trying to fill the sails or to get the boat to go anywhere in a straight line, sailors seem to have a language of their own. I know port from starboard and can recognise the bow from the stern but when Dad asks me to 'take the tiller' or 'change tack' I'm 'all at sea.' Everything on a boat has a special name—even the ropes aren't called ropes; they're lines or sheets depending on what they're attached to. Windward, leeward, boom, jib, roller-reefing, capstan, rudder, tacking, jibing—the list goes on.

'Keep it straight unless I tell you to move it,' he replied as

I took hold of the wooden tiller.

The 22-foot yacht gave a couple of rolls as the wind filled the sail, and I firmly grasped the tiller, in case Dad gave me sudden instructions to alter our course. Once Dad clambered back down across the deck, he adjusted the sails before switching off the outboard.

'I think there's enough wind to get the jib out,' he said, buzzing around the cockpit, doing about five things at once.

'Now we're sailing,' he yelled through a grin wider than the cut-mouth at the harbour entrance. His eyes flick to the GPS. 'Six and a half knots,' he said. 'The wind's blowing down the Forth,' he continued. 'We're before the wind.'

We effortlessly glided past the headland off Anstruther. The ever-strengthening wind ruffled through my hair. The sun was strong in the cloudless October sky, and I peered through my sunglasses, trying to picture the coastline I knew so well, which dominates the landscape.

Once settled, Dad sat beside me and relieved me of my steering duties. As well as the view from the top of Johnny Doo's, the landscape is seen from a different angle from a boat. Anstruther has always been a small fishing village to me, but you can't call it a fishing village anymore. The harbour is full of pontoons, luxury boats and motor-cruisers. There's not a fishing boat in sight. I stared to my northeast, trying to picture where Chalmers Church once stood. You could see the spire from miles away. The Craw's Nest, which should have been directly in front of us was the biggest and busiest hotel in Anstruther for over fifty years.

We were sailing along at a rate of knots. We'd almost

reached Billow Ness and Dad tried to spot Mum on the golf course. The further west we went, the same distance we had to sail back. We would be into the wind on our return, so a bit of tacking was required. Dad needed my help for this.

'Ok, what do you need me to do?'

'If you take the starboard side, I'll handle the port. We need to come about. The tide's coming in now and the wind has changed. When I tell you to, pull the sheet on your side until I tell you to stop. Remember to duck your head when the boom swings past.'

'Okay, no problem, Dad. ' I took the rope in my hand.

'Right, Billy, pull,' he said, pushing the tiller away from him.

I pulled the rope but had to use both hands as fast as I could to bring the sail in.

'Right, grab the tiller and keep it steady' he said, as the boat began to turn, and he started pulling on his side.

'You're doing great,' he said, as the yacht levelled out and we began to sail again.

Now the yacht was on an even keel, Dad popped into the cabin to get us each a coke.

'Shit, Dad!' I yelled as a strong gust caught the sails and suddenly spun the boat around.

He emerged from below, his eyes wide and a coke in each hand. Quickly realising the problem, he thrust the can in my general direction and scrambled up to rescue the sails. However, it was too late. The outer edge of the mainsail caught the rigging in the wind and ripped before Dad reached it. Our sail was over.

'I'm sorry Dad, I didn't expect that to happen. 'You should never ask a blind man to steer a boat.'

'It's okay, Billy, it can be fixed,' he said, motoring the rest of the way in.

I never sailed again unless Mum was with us.

~~~

In mid-July, Mum and Dad decided to take the boat out. The 27-foot McWester sat bobbing in the marina, as it had done all summer without leaving the harbour. Myakey 2—a new yacht they'd bought to upgrade the previous one creaked and moaned as the fenders rubbed against the jetty. Dad walked Dobby down to the boat several times to check on it. But it was the first time that Dobby had sailed with us. The gang-way wobbled as I made my way to the boat. Mum or Dad wouldn't let me fall in, but I took tentative steps approaching the yacht from the pontoon. Using my wheelchair was safer. Dobby jumped aboard.

Myakey 2 didn't have an outboard motor, but an engine which clanged and rattled under our feet. Dad manoeuvred the yacht far enough outside the harbour. Mum steered in the right direction as Dad raised the main sail. I was touching nothing… We set off towards the May Island—five miles from the harbour. I was anxious to know how Dobby would cope on a boat, but he was fine. We hooked his lead onto the rail just in case. If weather permitted, our aim was to sail around the island and back again. It is so peaceful on the water away from the hustle and bustle of normal day-to-day life. Dad often pushed me forward so he could grab the sheet on my
~~~

starboard side and haul it towards him. Mum operated the port side. We had a good wind for sailing and Captain Dobby sat staring out to sea. I often wondered why dogs stare out to sea! Apparently, they are inquisitive, and they are observing and learning about their surroundings. However, I had no concerns about Dobby jumping overboard. Although he was such a well-behaved dog throughout the trip, Dobby preferred it when we were back on dry land two hours later.

If it wasn't weather for sailing or the tides weren't right for going out, we often sat on the boat hobnobbing, relaxing with a drink and listening to the radio. Dobby followed his grandad everywhere. When Dad went ashore. When he disappeared down below. When Dad went to get our chippy tea, Dobby went with his grandad. He was like an elastic band attached to his grandad. He lay in the sun beside me. He lay beside his granny. But he still preferred lying with his grandad. In fact, Dobby enjoyed everyone's company.

Chapter 21

THE RESCUE

The Scottish Government eased lockdown restrictions further, allowing more people to meet indoors, but you still had to wear a face covering. We'd been wearing face coverings for some time now. Dobby didn't like it when his grandad arrived wearing a mask to take him for his walk. Dobby rarely barked but did so at his grandad. He found it strange that something was hiding his grandad's moustache.

'It's only me, you silly bugger,' he said, taking it off.

However, he soon got used to people wearing them. I had several of the things: a black one with an East Fife crest; a green and white; one my neighbour made out of old fabric for me; and a Gunners face mask that one of my mum's neighbours sent up from London. I had a colour for each team I supported. But I didn't like wearing masks because they impaired my vision. However, it was compulsory, especially in shops, hospitals and pubs.

Because Dobby was with me through lockdown, I was concerned about separation anxiety. There were the *Dreelside Shenanigans* when I left him on his own, but it wasn't enough. I needed to leave him for longer periods. I'd arranged to meet a friend in the Bank, so I left Dobby in the house on this occasion. I was happy to leave him because he was no longer chewing things in the house. I'd repaired the arm of the couch with a leather sofa repair kit—a sheet of brown adhesive leather. Once patched up, you couldn't tell the difference, and Dobby didn't touch it. I left the living room window open to give him some air. I was only a few yards away when I heard him whine. He still rarely barked. There was the odd time when he lay asleep, and if someone knocked on the door. Or if you didn't throw the ball for him. Apart from that, Dobby didn't bark. I had to keep walking. The whining faded the further away I got.

I judged how long it would take me to walk and arrive at the same time as Dave. I could have got the bus but avoided public transport while the virus was around. I'd timed it to perfection. Dave strolled up the street to meet me as I reached the Bank. We both fixed the elastic straps of our face masks around our lugs and entered. It was table service only, so once Dave had guided me into a seat, we removed our face coverings and waited on someone taking our order. You also had to leave your details for contact tracing in case there was an outbreak of Covid. I believe thousands of hospitality venues took advantage of the table service by adding an extra pound.

'How are you then, Dave?' I asked, raising my pint.

The walk down in the soaring July heat had made me thirsty and ready for a nice cold pint.

'Not bad, son,' he answered, having placed his pint of Tennents down.

Dave was one of the first guys I met when I went to St

Andrews on a regular basis. A short, stocky man with greying hair who liked a drink on his days off. I pictured him as a miniature Hagrid from *Harry Potter*—a gentle man with a full beard and small beetle-like eyes. However, Dave couldn't have been more different. A short, clean-shaven man with well-kept hair better describes him.

'Have you been up to much?' I asked.

'Not much to get up to, Billy son.'

'That's true. I've not been up to much myself. I'm glad we're getting out again.'

'I've not had a drink for four months,' Dave continued, taking another sip. 'I didn't miss it either.'

'You say that now, Dave, but once you get the taste for it again, you'll wonder how you went so long without a pint.'

'I've really not missed it,' he said again.

'I was the same. I mean, I've had the occasional drink in the house, but not what I used to have in the pub before lockdown. It's the company I miss.'

'I suppose you're right.'

'I had a pint in the Royal's beer garden a few weeks ago and enjoyed my first draft pint in months.'

Dave raised his hand, attracting a staff member.

'Same again, pal,' he called.

We were a short distance from the bar, so there was no need to summon the guy over. He promptly arrived with two fresh pints.

'I'll not stay for much longer,' I said. 'I've left Dobby in the house on his own and I've not left him much during the pandemic.'

'He'll make himself a cup of tea if he's thirsty,' Dave joked. 'How is he anyway?'

'Aye, he's good. We have a great relationship there. Bringing him up has been difficult, but I knew it would be.'

'You do well, son.'

'I like to think so,' I added, a wry smile forming on my lips as I took another drink.

'Look, I'm not going to be back at work anytime soon,' Dave began to gabble, as his tongue loosened. 'We can do this more often if you like. I can get a bus down easy enough.'

'That'll be good, Dave.'

After two rounds each, we filled out our contact details—Dave doing my one and called it a day. Four pints during the afternoon was probably too much for me knowing I had to walk home. As I approached the house, I listened for Dobby whining. But there wasn't any. When I unlocked, and opened the door, Dobby was waiting for his dad, his tail wagging in the air. And the house was how I left it.

'Good boy,' I said, collapsing on the couch, letting him jump all over his dad.

~~~

I was becoming more involved in the RNIB groups and joined extra ones as I learned about them. Someone who took part in the quiz told me about the Glasgow book group.

'Don't you have to be from Glasgow for that?' I asked.

'No, it's for anyone interested in books,' she replied.

I contacted my Connection Co-ordinator to find out more about the Glasgow book group. She asked the Connection
~~~

Co-ordinator for that area to get in touch with me. However, I learned quickly that the Glasgow book group wasn't for me. I felt like an outsider. Like I wasn't welcome. One member even asked, 'What are you doing in this group when you're not from Glasgow?'

'I was told you didn't have to be from Glasgow to join this group,' I said. 'And I like to read books,' I added.

'Where are you from?' another member asked.

I persevered, but realised it wasn't for me. There were a couple of people who were nice to me, but the majority couldn't care less. I found out why I didn't fit in. Most of the people in the group met up in Glasgow with their book club.

One of the groups I was fitting in nicely with was the football group.

One of the guys from the football call set up a zoom meeting for every Sunday evening. And this was mainly for Macar, Lewis, Jan, Claire and me. After a few weeks discussing football, we decided to meet up in Edinburgh for some drinks. Macar and Jan were used to pubs in the capital with both of them being Hibernian supporters. Macar chose the Middleton Bar on Easter Road because he was used to drinking there, and he was familiar with the staff. The reason for the venue was because its proximity to Waverley Station. Claire couldn't make it, so it was just the four of us.

Despite having no sight, Macar pre-booked the pub and taxi. He didn't arrange our train journeys, or passenger assistance, but he did contact Waverley to let them know there would be three blind people arriving at the station. I'd arranged my train times and assistance a few days before we travelled, but I was having second thoughts. I was going to be travelling on a train during the pandemic. I was visiting a busy city. And I was leaving Dobby with his granny and grandad for the night.

Mum or Dad wasn't keen to collect me from the train station when I got back, so gave me money to book Pro Taxi, a local firm to pick me up from the station. Eddie regularly picked me up from the pubs when I was out five nights a week, but I had rarely needed him since I got Dobby. I'd told Mum I wouldn't be late, but she insisted she pay for a taxi home to be on the safe side.

I fought back tears as the train door closed between Dobby and me. It was the first time Dobby watched his dad from a station platform being taken away in a train. Dad wheeled me onto the platform for my assistance to transfer me onto the train, but my wheelchair wasn't going. I arranged with the station guard to store it for coming back. Eddie would use it to wheel me back to his waiting taxi.

Pre-lockdown I had been used to train journeys. I travelled back and forth to the Royal National College for the Blind (RNC) in 2002/2003 and used them occasionally when I travelled for short stays at the Windermere Manor Hotel in the Lake District which used to be owned by Guide Dogs for the blind. I enjoyed visiting this hotel because a lot of blind and partially sighted people booked a stay at the Mannor, which meant I met many new people with blindness and sight loss. I was used to arranging passenger assistance for these trips. But during the pandemic was a new experience. Organising trains and booking assistance was the same, but I never thought I'd be travelling during a pandemic. However, I felt safer journeying this way than on a bus. As long as I kept my mask on and didn't touch anything, I would be fine.

The four of us arrived at Waverley around the same time and Jan was waiting to meet us. Jan had pretty good sight; Macar and Lewis had no sight. And I was severely sight impaired. It was handy for someone with vision to help. A taxi was waiting across the road, but we didn't know if it was ours, as the driver didn't get out to help. Jan confirmed it was for us, and we bundled ourselves in. The driver still made no attempt to help.

'That'll be nine pounds,' the driver said when we arrived at The Middleton.

'You're having a laugh, mate,' Macar protested. 'For that distance!'

I thought that price was reasonable for a city taxi.

'I'll be complaining to your company,' Macar continued.

'I'm sorry pal, but that's the price,' the driver replied.

I was staying out of it.

'I don't care. I'll be getting my money back,' he insisted, handing over his money.

'Sorry about that, mate,' I whispered. 'I've just met the guy.'

'No problem. I'm used to guys like him,' he whispered back.

Once in the pub, Macar phoned the company to complain about the service and the overpriced journey. They promised to refund him part of the fare. Now that was all sorted, we were able to relax with a drink.

Contact tracing forms lay on the table, but none of us were able to fill them in, so the barman assisted. Lewis and Macar both had a vodka and Red Bull. Jan opted for a Kopparberg, while I had my usual pint. I only planned to have two and then go onto whisky and lemonade because I was in a strange environment and didn't want to have to find my way to the toilet too often, but knew I would have to go eventually.

The pub was busy, but not so loud that you couldn't have a conversation without having to raise your voice. The pub also smelled thick with stale cigarette smoke; the smell seems to hang in the air and drift into the building.

A large flat screen telly was on in the corner showing the Community Shield match between Arsenal and Liverpool. Though an Arsenal fan, I didn't pay much attention to it because I was with friends. The English Premiership had been catching up by showing every game live every day to get the season finished. The Community Shield meant the new season would start the following weekend.

I used my ears to see what direction people were going to the toilet. Jan assisted Lewis and Macar to the male toilet, but they were on their own after that. But there was usually someone to help. When I needed, I went unaided. It was easy enough running my long cane along the edge of the bar, and once I ran out of bar, the toilet was on the right. And like Lewis and Macar, someone offered to help.

I enjoyed my day with my friends but, like always, I missed Dobby. I was sure he was having a ball with his granny and grandad while his dad was having a great time in Edinburgh. We each got one round of drinks and had something to eat from the chippy across the road. I opted for a sausage supper, something easy to eat using my fingers.

'Yuk, Macar, you didn't just let that woman dig her fingers into your box for a chip?'

'Yes, mate.'

'You don't know where her fingers have been,' I said.

There was no chance they were getting any of my chips. They could keep their grubby fingers to themselves. Covid or not, I have never been fond of anyone fingering anything that I eat.

The same taxi firm arrived back for us, and this driver was a little more helpful. Despite Macar making a hullabaloo over the first guy, the fare was still nine pounds. I handed the driver a tenner and told him to keep the change. I've always tipped a taxi driver. We all said our goodbyes before our assistance people took us away to our respective trains.

My train was on time as it slowed to a halt at Leuchars station where Eddie was waiting with my wheelchair.

'D'you have a good time?' he asked as he wheeled me along the bridge.

'Aye, it was good,' I said through my mask.

The flashing lights of Eddie's taxi dazzled my eyes as we approached. He helped me in, and we were on our way.

'What was it you were away to today for?' he asked.

'I was meeting up with friends I've met through the RNIB,' I explained, raising my voice so he could hear me through the Perspex divide.

'That's good then,' he said.

'Aye, they're good people,' I added. 'I sort of brought our

taxi runs to an abrupt end when I got Dobby, Eddie,' I went on.

'That's okay, don't worry about it. How is he getting on, anyway?'

'Aye, he's great. It was tough to begin with, but he's grown out of doing a lot of things he's not meant to do.'

'Our Jack Russell was like that. He used to steal things, but he doesn't anymore and he's eighteen now.'

'That's a good age, Eddie.'

'The thing about Jack Russells is that you can never tire them out.'

'That's for sure. Dobby's always on the go. He's a wee attention seeker.'

'Mum and Dad have him tonight?'

'Aye, they do, but I said, there'll be no point in keeping him because I will be home early enough. But I think Dad wanted to keep him.'

'I see your dad walking him a lot.'

'Yeah, he loves that dog. He'd walk him all of the time if he could. Mum walks him a lot, too.'

'I've seen you walk Dobby, too. You do well.'

'Thanks, Eddie.'

'Do you think this virus will go away anytime soon?' he asked, changing the subject.

'No, I don't think so.'

'Me neither. I think this virus will be around longer than me,' he said.

'Aye, I think so. I don't think places will re-open until a vaccine is available.'

'If places open at all,' Eddie added.

It felt like the time when I went to St Andrews for a night out in November the previous year when I got home about half an hour later. I still found it difficult when I opened the door to an empty house. I had been so used to Dobby greeting me when I came home, his tail swishing through the air, walloping against the kitchen bin. The only consolation I had was that Dad promised to bring Dobby back in the morning, rather than keep him until mid-day like the last time Mum and Dad had kept him overnight.

~~~

The weather turned as we moved into September and Dobby's Gotcha day was fast approaching. It was a lot cooler by the time Dobby's party came around. I was expecting around twenty guests, including family members, a few of the *Dreelside Shenanigans* and some dogs. After all, the party was for Dobby.

Dad was in charge of the barbecue, among other chores. A couple of my neighbours came round in the morning to help Dad erect my gazebo. This was placed over the wall which Dad built—giving it extra cover if it rained; and going by the overcast sky, this was likely. Dobby was curious, watching this strange thing being put up.

'Will one gazebo be enough?' Lynne, my neighbour, and a member of the *Dreelside Shenanigans* asked, once it was up.

She was right… I was expecting lots of people and quite a bit of the garden was uncovered.

'We only have one,' Dad replied.
~~~

'I've got one in my shed,' Lynne said, inspecting the rest of the garden space. 'The other gazebo will fit nicely where the shed was.'

'If that's no bother,' Dad said.

'No bother at all.' Lynne disappeared to fetch her own one.

She promptly arrived back with her gazebo, and once that was up, it did look a lot better. The barbecue was set up in the corner between the gazebos. Because it was colder, Mum was concerned about people getting cold bums on the little wall, so organised padded bench rolls to be brought up from the yacht. Those who were able to, brought their own deck chairs.

Time was running out and we still had lots of preparation to do. Mum brought up her table she used for occasions such as these. She made sure all the glasses were washed and dried. She brought extra glasses up. She made sure there was plenty of prosecco chilling, including using my small beer fridge, and her portable fridge.

I was busy making sure my music playlist was going to work. I unplugged the echo device and moved it closer to the kitchen window and connected it to my Bluetooth speaker. I made sure the optic stand had enough bottles on it. Dobby and I were ready to receive guests. I wanted a bottle of sanitiser taped to the garden gate, so people sanitised before entering.

However, Mum implied that people would decide to sanitise if they wanted to, so placed a bottle on each table.

My next-door neighbours were first to arrive, and Dobby padded to the gate to greet them. Dobby knew something was going on with all of these new things happening and many people starting to arrive. A lot of my guests brought their own prosecco, which was nice, and added to the many bottles I already had, but I wasn't expecting people to arrive with gifts for Dobby.

A lot of the gifts included dog treats, and I didn't like to say he doesn't get them. Dobby licked his lips in front of someone eating a sausage. He wagged his tail at someone else sucking on a strawberry tart, hoping for dropped crumbs. And wandering hands sneaked him a crisp from their plate.

Some guests, despite knowing not to feed Dobby, did anyway. Flushed faces gave the guilty parties away when being told off. Dobby knew not to come to me for food because I trained him to lie down when his dad is cooking or eating.

Most of the *Dreelside Shenanigans* came round. Mary, who owned the Maltese crossed with a chihuahua called Teddy, left him at home. After some of us convinced her to go and get him, she did. Dobby now had a cocker spaniel and a malchi to play with. All three dogs got on well with each other and were close in age.

I let my music play on shuffle while everyone was enjoying themselves—having a laugh and chatting away. I didn't tell anyone the music was playing from my echo device because I didn't want people shouting at it, asking, 'Alexa, play…'

The day rolled into night. People came and went. I never exceeded the number of people you were allowed at one time. The barbecue was a roaring success with all food cooked and eaten. Bottles of prosecco were still being popped. Mum left the opened bottles on the table for everyone to help themselves. Plates of crisps were passed round, but I refused. I've never been a fan of sharing crisps. I've been particularly cautious since Covid, but it's a phobia I've had for many years. If I want crisps, I'll eat a packet by myself.

The party began to die down as people went home, but there were still a few of us left. And the ones who remained huddled under the one gazebo. It rained later, but it wasn't heavy. Dad put my Bluetooth speaker inside to save it from getting damaged in the rain, despite it being waterproof. It was a long day for Dobby. While we continued drinking into the night, he lay flat out on the bench roll.

There were only five of us left when my next-door neighbours decided to go home at half past two in the morning. The first to arrive and the last to leave. There was a lot to clean up, but Mum and Dad told me not to touch anything and they would do it all in the morning. It had been a long day for all of us, especially for Mum and Dad who'd been on their feet all day and rarely stopped, making sure everyone else was happy. They, as well as Dobby and I needed a right good rest.

A few days after the party, Mum came to walk Dobby as normal. Since I had learned everyone was walking Dobby off the lead, I asked them not to because I didn't think he was ready yet. Mum and Uncle Weh obliged, but Dad would not adhere to my request. He always did what he thought was right.

I remember one night, after tea at Mum's, Dad and I went in opposite directions. He started walking Dobby one way, while I walked up the road on my own. Usually, I arrived home about ten minutes before Dad and Dobby, but I was almost home when a small, white dog appeared in front of me.

Dobby had seen me, so Dad let him off the lead and he galloped to greet me. I waited until Dad caught up.

'What've you got him off the lead for?' I asked, waiting for a reply that I already had a comeback for.

'He walks fine off the lead,' he said.

'I know he's fine off the lead, Dad, but I've told you umpteen times, he's not ready. Especially along a main road.'

'But he's good walking along…'

'I don't care, Dad. You get on at me about walking Dobby along a main road.'

'But that's different.'

'How is it?'

'You can't see if there's another dog. He might run across the road to see that dog.'

'No, Dad, if he sees another dog, he'll stop and whine, but he'll not attempt to pull me across the road. He's not finished his training yet, anyway.'

'Aye, okay,' he said, approaching the house.

Dobby was, indeed, good at walking off the lead, and was very streetwise, but until I was ready, I wanted everyone to keep him on the lead.

Mum walked Dobby for half an hour, the time I requested because the recommended walking time for a Jack Russell is half an hour, twice a day. But one day Mum was gone a lot longer. What had happened to them?

Mum arrived back about an hour and twenty minutes after she had left with Dobby.

'Sorry we've been so long,' Mum said panting and out of

breath.

'That's okay. I was just getting a bit worried, that's all.'

'Dobby's been quite the hero, haven't you, Dobs,' she said, catching her breath.

'Oh, have you really, pal?' I said, stroking his belly. 'What have you done with Granny to make you a hero then?'

'Well, you know the woman with the two whippets?'

'Aye, Jean.'

I often met Jean, a woman in her early seventies, who regularly walked two whippets. She sometimes let one of them off the lead to play with Dobby but kept hold of the other one. Whippets are known for their speed, but Dobby was a close match. Despite having small legs, Dobby can keep up with most dogs. And he can leave most bigger dogs behind because he turns quicker.

'Well, I met her up the park and she was in hysterics. Her dogs had run off. I said I would look out for them. Well, did I not find them!'

'Where were they?'

'They were up The Milton.'

The Milton is a field at the back, in between Anstruther and Pittenweem—a popular route for walking dogs.

'It was too far to go back and let Jean know. They were looking around for her.'

'What was that?' I asked, waiting for the rest of the story.

'I'm sorry, I know you don't want us to walk Dobby off the lead, but I had to do something. He's very good walking off the lead so I unclipped it and approached the whippets.'

'You approached another dog,' I was beginning to laugh

a little.

'Shut up, it's not funny,' she said, continuing her tale. 'They had their collars on, so I used Dobby's lead, threaded it through the collar of both dogs and walked them back to Jean. Dobby walked all the way back off his lead.'

'Quite the rescue then. Not bad for someone who doesn't like dogs.'

'I couldn't leave them.'

'I know Dobby's good off the lead now. I meant, I don't want him off the lead near busy roads, but as long as there is no danger, then it's fine.'

A box of chocolates lay on Mum's doorstep a week later. It didn't have a note, but she learned they were from Jean to say thanks for rescuing her dogs.

~~~

Fiona began contacting everyone during August to let them know classes would recommence in September. She was receiving regular updates on when to expect the hall to re-open. Certain protocols were put in place, which included one owner per dog. Of course, there would be exemptions for me, and Mum or Dad were allowed to assist.

Fiona sent all guidelines prior to classes and asked if Dobby was coming back to complete his silver award. Dobby had a lot of training at home and plenty of attention, but further training would help—especially re-call. I still struggled to call him into the house. Sometimes, the only way I managed to get him to come in was if I opened the living room door to the hall and bedroom, looked to the garden towards him,
~~~

and head into the bedroom. I would hear little paws thunder along the floor. Once he was past me, I hurried to close the back door. A lengthy telling off would follow.

Dad was still busy with his customers, but Mum wasn't so much. This meant Dad couldn't take me to training, so Mum had to. She dreaded the time when she would have to take me on her own.

There was only an hour of daylight left when Mum pulled up in her van outside the Erskine Hall. Dobby still didn't like the car, but he was happy with the van. Each session was fifteen minutes shorter, so, there was a new start time of quarter to seven—giving the previous class of dogs time to exit and gave Fiona time to clean before the next set of dogs. This suited Mum, as she didn't have to get us out of the van and chat to other people. She watched as the previous class left.

'I'm glad we weren't in that class,' Mum said, helping me out of the van.

'Why's that, Mum?' I asked, as I swung my feet out.

'Some bloody big dogs just left that hall!'

'I'm sure they wouldn't hurt you,' I said, waiting for her getting Dobby out. 'Mind you though, you never know with your track record.'

'Aye, you can say that again.'

Mum was still wary of dogs having been bitten by them three times when she was younger.

Despite Mum timing it right, we stood socially distanced outside waiting for Fiona to call us in. Dobby didn't pull when he was on walks with me, but seeing dogs he hadn't seen for a while, it was natural for him to want to speak to old and new friends. Once Dobby stopped saying hello to everyone, and Fiona beckoning us in, Mum guided us to the seats which were side-by-side, set out for us.

The rest of the seats were a metre apart from each other. The class was reduced by half, but some of the same dogs were present, including Katie, the big black border collie. Dobby gave a pitiful squeal, as Katie was the last dog he went to kiss, and she bit him. Maybe Mum was right to fear dogs, but it was just a warning from Katie and Dobby was fine.

Fiona stood in her usual position on the stage, instructing the class.

'Welcome back everybody,' she began, waving her arms, calling for some hush. 'You should all, by now, have your dog microchipped, have identification and be registered with a vet. Some of your dogs might be rusty, but the silver award should help to reconnect with the basics and learn new advanced training skills.'

Fiona came round as she always did before starting and greeted each dog and their owner.

'Hello, Dobby,' Fiona said, when she reached us. 'How are you, pal?' she asked, handing him a treat.

Fiona had to be professional because she had a class to run and be impartial to each dog, but I had been in contact with her over the summer, asking her for advice if I needed any. I arranged for her to come and take Dobby out for me if Mum and Dad were away. So, I think Dobby was her favourite.

'Okay,' she said, returning to her position on the stage, like a woman on a mission. 'We'll see where you all are by starting with the controlled walk. Just as before, walking around the hall.'

I was a lot more comfortable with this exercise now having walked a lot with Dobby on my own. The one concern I had was that Dobby might behave differently with other dogs in the hall. But he wasn't because he was so focused on his dad's guidance, having walked regularly with me.

'Clever boy,' I told him, walking around the hall.

Mum walked a short distance behind us, trusting me with Dobby. Perhaps yellow markers were on the floor before, but I hadn't noticed them; because they were yellow against blue, they were easier for me to see.

'Okay,' Fiona called. 'If you head back to your seats.'

Mum guided us to ours.

'That was really good,' Fiona said. 'The exercises will get trickier, but that was good.'

The tasks did indeed get harder, but nothing I didn't think Dobby and I couldn't master. I had a look at some of the tasks which we would be expected to carry out, and most of them were manageable.

However, I didn't concentrate enough on asking Dobby to lie down or stand. This might cause a problem when I put him through his gold certificate. But that was some way off. There were other tasks to tackle first. The reason why getting him to lie, sit or stand was so important was because Fiona told us to stop walking and tell our dog to sit, lie or stand when instructed. And we didn't get the choice. This would be standard to pass the gold certificate. You had to leave your dog in the same position for a period of time without the dog moving.

When Fiona asked us to carry out a simpler task, which was to play with your dog, I dropped to my knees and started to wrestle with him. But no play fighting was allowed—a pity, because we liked a good wrestle.

The last, and always the most difficult task is the re-call. I hoped he would be better at it by now, but he wasn't. He did approach more when I called him, but he got halfway and darted to another dog. It was still a work in progress. I should have been able to do this by now. I'd had Dobby for over a year now. I was kicking myself that I hadn't cracked it.

'What are you trying him with at home?' Fiona asked.

'Shouting on him. Showing a ball. Patting my thighs. Anything to get him in the house.'

'Okay, try something he doesn't usually get. Praise him if he comes in for it. See if that works.'

'Okay, I'll give it a try.'

Our first session back went okay, and Mum was really good at helping. The following week would be a controlled walk outside and unlike before, when Dad took the lead and did this on my behalf, I was going to do it this time. I also tried some things Fiona suggested to get Dobby to come in.

I sat in the living room, took out a digestive biscuit, held it in sight and called him in. He ran towards me, took the offered snack and ran out again. Shaking my head, I muttered, 'C'mon Dobby, do this for Dad, please.

I cut up cubes of cheese and kept it in a bag in the fridge. I sat on my kitchen seat and opened the fridge door. I took the bag out and called on him. He came in and I asked him to sit. Once he did, I took a piece from the bag and held it out. He looked at me, then glanced towards the door and back at me. I swung the door closed and gave him his treat.

'Good boy,' I said, giving his head a stroke.

The more I did this, the more he came in and he got his reward.

Chapter 22

FUN AND GAMES

A metallic blue MG pulled alongside our Mitsubishi as we made our way along the A720 Edinburgh bypass towards Musselburgh. Dad chuckled when he glanced to his left.

'What's so funny?' I asked, holding Dobby on my lap.

'He's laughing at the woman in the car beside us,' Mum interjected from the back seat.

The woman driving the MG had been looking at us and had seen Dobby's nose squashed against the passenger-side window. She gave a broad grin at Dobby's little face, his chin resting on the sill. Dobby sat on my lap, a carabiner—a metal clip attached to his collar and the seatbelt, as we both stared out of the window at the MG. The alloyed wheels spun like a Catherine wheel.

I pictured the woman with long wavy blonde hair and sunglasses perched on her nose. The woman, around my age, had high cheekbones with a tanned complexion. I visualised her with bright red lipstick and grey eyes behind her shades. The MG faded into the distance.

We had bought a dog guard for the car in January. He was barely tall enough to see over the back seats. Mum and

I had still been taking Dobby to different places to walk him when he was younger. She often took us for a run in the car and stopped for lunch. We had been to the Common or Pittenweem. We ate our food on the pier where *Miakey 2* sat. Although Dobby disliked the car, we teased him and tried to get him to enjoy car journeys.

'Dobbbyyy,' Mum encouraged.

There was no response.

'Dobbbyyy,' I added my voice, seeing if it made a difference. It didn't. However, we kept trying.

'Dobbbyyy,' Mum tried again.

His little head popped through the gap in the seats.

'There we go,' she said through a mouthful of panini.

'Dobbbyyy!' He had disappeared again.

He reappeared with a smile on his face.

The more we tried, the better he was. We ended up taking the guard away because I didn't like placing him in the boot of the car.

The following week after dog training recommenced, Katie's owner was waiting for us. She approached when we exited the van.

'I apologise for last week,' she said. 'I don't know what came over Katie.'

'That's okay,' I replied. 'It's because they've not seen each other for a while. And he's fine.'

'All the same, I've got something for Dobby.' She handed over a bag.

'You're not needing to do that,' Mum offered, accepting the bag.

'It's nothing—only some treats and a toy.'

'There's no need,' Mum said again.

'But thanks for that,' I said, with a broad smile. 'Dobby will enjoy ripping the toy apart.'

Despite Fiona saying that the controlled walk would be outside that week, it wasn't. We performed the usual tasks inside. We did do the controlled walk outside the following week, and to save time, Mum and I arranged to meet everyone else at the start of Bankie Park. Because Dobby was used to walking with his dad all summer, it was a piece of cake. Dobby and I took the lead, which meant everyone else walked at a slower pace, behind us.

But according to Fiona, this was a good thing because they had to be in more control of their dog. When we got so far, she asked us to turn around and the shoe was on the other foot. We were behind everyone else, and I had to make sure Dobby didn't pull me trying to keep up with the dogs in front. Fortunately, Dobby learned not to pull his dad and the only time he did was when he needed a poop. He found a spot on the grass verge and dumped it there. Mum told me to keep going while she picked it up.

The rest of the tasks were performed inside, and they were pretty much the same. And, as usual, the re-call was last. He was making progress with this.

The rest of September's and the beginning of October's training was going well apart from getting Dobby to stay in the position Fiona requested. He still didn't have a problem sitting when instructed, but he didn't lie down or stand. Fiona taught us to do this with a treat. You hold the treat out in front of him so that he's focused on it. You then gradually lower it to the floor and ask him to lie. You raise the treat in the air for him to sit or stand. I just couldn't master it. One of the tasks he would be required to do in order to pass his silver certificate was to jump into a car, stay comfortable for a few minutes and when told, jump out again. Fiona used her boot to do this. He never jumped into our car willingly, but he didn't hesitate with Fiona's one. He had a good sniff around before jumping out again.

We were going to miss the penultimate week of training before his exam.

Mum and Dad's holidays are spent sunning themselves by a pool or beach, usually in Portugal or the Spanish Islands. They had been due to go to Fuerteventura in the previous summer but had cancelled the trip because of Covid. They looked at alternative staycations closer to home. My holidays abroad were over—for the time being, anyway. I hadn't been abroad for the past few years and the last time I did was my European road trip with my two friends in 2016. Dad looked for pet-friendly holidays in the UK and found Drummohr Holiday Lodges near Edinburgh, a peaceful, picturesque, sheltered site in East Lothian. The property he found was a fully furnished self-catering two-bedroomed lodge with a hot tub. It was ideal for all of us.

A few days before we were due to go to Musselburgh, my dad took Dobby for a run along Billow Ness beach. His little legs nimbly jump from rock to rock. His nose can easily source out something he shouldn't.

'He ate a green crab down the beach,' Dad announced when he brought Dobby home. 'I tried to stop him, but I couldn't get to him in time.'

Crabs have to be cooked alive. You can hear squeals coming from the boiling pan. Apparently, it's air escaping from their shell. Dead, uncooked crabs are poisonous.

'We'll just have to hope he's okay,' I replied.

With a sensitive stomach like Dobby's, he constantly went to the back door two days before we travelled. He ran to the door, hurried to me and back to the door—signs that he needed out. I held him to my chest.

'Please be okay for Monday,' I said, stroking his head.

We thought he'd dried up by Monday morning but Dad, while I took a shower, found a dollop of diarrhoea on the doormat when he came to walk him. Dad alerted me by shouting through the bathroom door.

My first holiday in years and Dobby was ill. All of that money was going to be wasted. Dobby's health was more important than a holiday. Did he have to choose to be ill now, I questioned, letting the water cascade over me.

'What will we do?' I yelled back.

'We can't go when he's like that,' Dad said over the noise of running water.

'We can't cancel. It's too late now.' I thumped the off switch on the shower.

'Okay, I'll pop to the vet in St Andrews and see if they'll give me something for him.'

Once dressed, I paced around my bedroom while Dad was away. My elbows rested on the kitchen table, my head in my hands. I could hear Dobby playing in the garden waiting for his grandad.

Dad returned a short time later with medication.

'Right,' he began, reading the instructions. 'We've to give him two doses of this *Vetpro Digestive* stuff today, then one dose for two days.'

'Okay, that's good,' I said, brushing my palm across my brow. 'Is there anything else?'

'Aye, the receptionist said to feed him small amounts of bland food.'

'What did she mean by bland?'

'White food such as scrambled egg. Chicken. Boiled rice and boiled fish.'

'Oh right. And that'll dry him up?'

'It should do, aye. I'll nip along to the fish shed and get a couple of bits of haddock.'

'What if it doesn't work?' I prompted.

'She said to contact a local vet in Musselburgh if he's still not right.'

Dobby's illness wasn't serious, so we didn't have to cancel our holiday.

We were later in leaving than planned, but with the car packed, along with my wheelchair and dog, we were on our way for Dobby's first holiday. The gravel crunched and groaned under the wheels of our four-wheeled drive when we pulled up in front of our lodge. We arrived around mid-after-noon, and a staff member showed us to our lodge by driving in front. We could have found it ourselves but perhaps it was Covid protocol. The man jumped out and showed Mum and Dad inside. Dobby and I waited in the car until one of them returned.

'Just you sit there, Billy,' Dad said, opening the car door and lifting out Dobby. 'I'll get everything inside and come and get you.'

'Aye, okay,' I replied.

I would have preferred to go in with them so I could suss the place out, but I sat and had a cigarette while Mum and Dad were being shown around. Dad often left me in the car and let me know where everything was after they'd been in. Dad still didn't understand the nature of my blindness. With every other setting, I work out things quickly. I'd not long dropped my cigarette butt on the gravel when Dad returned.

I heard feet crunching before Dad said, 'Right, Billy, I'll get you inside.'

'If you need anything, don't hesitate to contact the office,' the man said, climbing back into his car.

Dad guided me to a set of four wooden steps I had to negotiate before entering the lodge. The place was freezing, as I began walking around. All windows were open to circulate the air—blowing away Covid I guess, in case the previous occupants had had the virus. It wasn't difficult. The lodge had a large open-plan kitchen with table and chairs as you entered. A sitting area was on the opposite side next to the patio doors. And in between the two, a small hallway led to the bedrooms and toilet. My room had two single beds with an ensuite wet-floor shower room. Dobby followed his dad through, jumped onto a bed and started to rub his body along it.

Once the car was unpacked and Mum and Dad were satisfied I could find my way around, we settled ourselves down and Dad picked up the welcome pack. Dobby lay beside him as he thumbed through the pages.

'You must keep your dog off the furniture and bedding at all times,' Dad read, lifting his head to glance at Dobby lying beside him.

'Well, he's already broken that rule,' I said.

'We'll just have to try from now on,' Dad replied as I sensed a flicker of a grin behind the brochure.

'Like we're going to stop him from doing that. He thinks that's the natural thing to do because that's what he does at home,' I added.

'Shepherd's pie okay for tea tonight?' Mum asked, interrupting the debate.

'Aye, that's fine,' both Dad and I said at the same time.

Mum began preparing the pie, while Dad continued browsing the pack. Dad usually sat and looked at everything on our arrival. He liked to find out what was in the surrounding area.

'The pie will take a while, so do the pair of you fancy a soak in the hot tub?' Mum asked, placing the dish in the oven.

The second I heard the word hot tub; I made my way to change into my trunks. Mum and Dad were ready before me, but I needed help to get in, so Dad obliged. Balancing is tricky, so I had to work out the best way of getting in. After a little deliberation, I turned myself around on the second step and sat my bum on the edge. I took a hold of Dad's shoulder, lifted my right leg over with my free hand, slid along and lifted my other leg over. A difficult process, but I got there. It felt like I'd just plunged into a large pot of boiling water. The elation was instant. I sat, allowing my muscles to relax as I remembered the previous experiences in a hot tub.

We had celebrated my dad's sixtieth in 2017 in a Vegas Spa plus lodge in Piperdam—a leisure resort, a few miles outside Dundee. The lodge slept up to twelve people, so it was perfect for large gatherings. Mum and Dad, along with my auntie, uncle and their friends, had been to Piperdam before. I, on the other hand, hadn't been. Not appreciating what Piperdam was, I spent my usual weekend in the pubs. One of my cousins met me in The Anstruther Boat House and asked why I wasn't at Piperdam. She and her family were heading up to join them the next day. If I'd known what it was, I would have gone.

The place was stunning! The lodge had four double bedrooms and two single rooms on the ground floor. A staircase led up to a fully equipped kitchen, lounge and a large games room with a snooker table, roulette table and multiple decks of cards and gambling chips. Outside was our own private hot tub. I was reluctant to go in, but with the help from my brother, I'm glad I did. It felt strange sitting in steamy water with other people, but they were family and friends.

My second experience of a lodge was to bring in the new year in December of the same year. This time, it was just our family—Mum, Dad, Michael, my niece and nephew. However, Michael took Mya and Mikey home on the thirtieth and returned to join us. The snow gently fell just before midnight. We'd never spent New Year away. It was two degrees outside, but forty degrees in the tub as we sipped our drinks—all four faces flushed as we had been in too long. I noticed the benefits. My breathing felt better. My legs were relaxed and more supple and my general health improved. After our New Year away, I was hooked. I wanted a hot tub of my own. And my heart was set on getting one that year.

Mum and Dad were on board with the idea, but they had concerns.

'D'you realise how much it costs to run a hot tub?' Dad asked one evening.

'Yes,' I retorted, taking a deep breath.

'D'you think you'll manage that?' Mum asked. 'And what about getting in and out?'

They were right. I needed help to get in and out when we were away. So how would I manage? The conversation continued.

'I'll be fine, don't worry.'

'I'll do nothing but worry,' Mum said. 'I'm not wanting to arrive in the morning and find you face down in the bloody thing.'

'You get adaptations for them.'

'And what about when you come home from the pub?' Dad interjected.

'The reason for wanting a hot tub, Dad, is to not go to the pub as often. And do you really think I would be stupid enough to go in it when I'm drunk?'

'But like your mum said, it'll be too expensive.'

'I'll manage.'

'I think it will be too expensive to run,' Mum continued.

'And your garden is too exposed. We'll do nothing but worry, but if you're sure it's what you want.'

'Aye, it is.'

Things were not rolling along as I expected. By the middle of the summer, I was no further forward. I had a spot picked out in the garden where there was plenty of room. Dad eventually took me to look at hot tubs. We travelled far and wide to find a suitable one. We finally settled on one from a company in Falkirk. The man was helpful and picked one out which would be ideal for me—a small tub which sat four people.

'What about adaptations?' I asked.

'What kind of adaptations?' he replied.

'Can you fit grab handles?'

'Yeah, if that'll help you, then sure.'

I still needed time to work out how, and if I was actually going to afford one but I would find a way.

I arranged an electrician to install an outside, waterproof plug. By a stroke of luck my new neighbours had two large dogs and demanded the council give them a higher fence. This way, my garden would be completely enclosed. Then I blew it.

After a family night out to celebrate my graduation, we arrived back at my house. As I stumbled through the gate, I lifted my left crutch and waved it in the air.

'If I had my hot tub, I'd be in it by now,' I slurred, fumbling for my keys.

Discussions about getting a hot tub died down. I wondered why. So, I asked Dad when walking home from Mum and

Dad's after tea one night.

'When are we going for my hot tub, Dad?'

'We're not.'

'What d'you mean we're not?'

'You're not getting one.'

'Why?'

'Because of what you said the other week. We can't trust you to not come home from the pub and go in the hot tub.'

'That's not what I meant, and you know that,' I said, through gritted teeth. 'I only meant that if I had it, I would have already been in it, not when I got home from the pub.'

'You're not getting one and that's that!'

Dobby pottered around, investigating his surroundings while we sat sipping our drinks in the hot tub in Musselburgh and we chatted in the tub. I was satisfied sitting with Mum and Dad, and happy going in when they did. They could bring drinks out and they felt better helping me in and out. It was probably safer I didn't get one after all. It was better with a dog instead. We encouraged him to come and see us and he did. He stood on his hind legs and rested his front paws on the side, but he wasn't tall enough to see over the rim. We all laughed at his little face looking up at us. Forty minutes was long enough, so we got ourselves out and changed for tea.

We had a few drinks watching the telly before going to bed. Mum and Dad were often early to bed, and since I had got Dobby, so was I. However, when we're away, I tend to stay up later because Dad stays up with me to make sure I get to my bed and turn the lights out, despite my telling him I am perfectly capable of doing those things myself. I didn't like to keep Dad up too long, so I headed to bed. I hoped Dobby would come with me.

Dobby's bed was in the living room, but he didn't lie in it. A different place was strange for him, and he didn't know what to do. We also had to be vigilant in case he needed out during the night. I lay listening to little paws pad around the lodge. He stopped outside Mum and Dad's room. He came and jumped up beside me. A few minutes later, he jumped off and stood at Mum and Dad's door again. I heard him pad back to the living room. He began to whine outside Mum and Dad's room again.

'Dobby, come through here beside Dad,' I moaned, as I tried to fall asleep.

It was going to be a long night, as he repeatedly wandered back and forth. This had to stop. We couldn't have this all night.

'Dad,' I yelled.

'What is it?' he called back.

'I think Dobby needs out.'

I heard shuffling feet, and the door opened. Dad took him outside, but he didn't do anything. He needed attention.

'He's just going to pine for you all night,' I said when they returned.

'Okay, I'll sleep in your room.'

Dobby was happier. He was more settled, curled up beside his grandad. I couldn't sleep for Dad snoring, his throat clucking. For him blowing. How anyone can sleep in the same room as Dad is beyond me.

Dad was up first, so took Dobby for his walk. All walking

duties were Dad's when we were away. We also left him in charge of Dobby's food and medication. By the time I got up, Mum and Dad were already in the tub. I heard the whirring of the motor because the hot tub was on the other side of my room. I grabbed my trunks which had been drying on the towel rail, put them on and went to join them.

'Why d'you not tell me you were going in the hot tub?' I asked shuffling myself outside.

'We weren't waking you,' Mum giggled, holding a glass of something.

'What's that you're drinking?' I asked, once Dad helped me in.

'A Bucks Fizz,' she replied. 'You want one?'

'Of course.'

Dad got out to fetch me one before jumping back in.

'How is Dobby this morning?' I asked, reaching for my glass.

'Watch and not knock that over,' Dad said, watching me feel for my drink. 'He's no better,' he explained.

'At least he's had no more accidents,' I said.

'Aye, but his poops are like water.'

Gulping, I said, 'If he's no better in the morning, I want to take him to a local vet.'

'Aye, okay,' Dad agreed.

Dobby was, apart from his loose stool, fine in himself—although it didn't help that bags of my medication lay on the coffee table, and he ripped my bag open. The last thing we needed was for him to swallow human pills. Thankfully, they were all still there.

Dad made breakfast after we'd spent time in the tub and by the time we'd showered and eaten, it was almost mid-morning. Because there was nothing wrong with Dobby's fitness, we decided to take a run in the car to find a park. Dad spotted one somewhere on the way in, and it was only a couple of minutes' drive. Despite Dad taking him for his morning and evening walks, I needed to keep my end up, so I wanted to walk him when we got to the park. I attached him to my belt as usual and began walking. Mum and Dad stayed behind to keep me right and wheeled my chair behind in case I needed to rest.

We found a large clearing and plenty of room to throw a ball. I unclipped him and pulled the ball from my pocket. I waved it in front of him. He jumped up and down on his hunkers like a leaping gazelle with his mouth open wide. I threw it as far as I could and watched him pelt after it. His little legs thundered along the grass again like the hoof beats of miniature horses. I held out my hand waiting for him to return. He dropped it in front of me. He was good at bringing the ball straight to me but didn't always drop it into my hand.

There were a few people in the distance to my left and dogs with them, but as long as Dobby was focused on the ball, he didn't bother about them. Sometimes, if he caught a scent of something, he dropped the ball and didn't bring it back. Mum or Dad had to get it. Dobby had fun playing with his dad, granny and grandad, but after about half-an-hour, we headed back to the car.

The trip away was meant to be a relaxing one so we headed back to the lodge. Mum had packed a few games to keep us occupied, including dominos, a pack of large print playing cards, large print Scrabble and Monopoly. Mum prepared some sandwiches before we sat at the kitchen table to play Scrabble. Dobby wasn't quite right because the exertions in the park had taken it out of him and he lay in his bed. Dad was giving him his bland food and medication. I looked over to him sleeping. Sleeping was something that he barely did when he was energetic: something was going on. It wasn't like him. He was going to have to go to the vet's.

'Is it too early for a drink?' Dad asked, after making sure Dobby was okay.

'No,' Mum answered, setting up the board.

'We're on holiday,' I said, looking closely at a tile, trying to make out which letter it was.

I hadn't played any of these games for years and it wasn't until I tried to play them now that I realised again how much eyesight I'd lost. The game took an age because I struggled to see the letters. Mum and Dad helped by telling me what word they'd put down and what letters I could attach my word to. I picked up a tile, held it close to my eye and threw it down. One game was enough.

We attempted cards instead, but the large print suits and numbers weren't large enough either. Something I didn't need my eyes for, like quizzes, would have been better but we hadn't brought any.

Mum didn't cook every night while we were away, so instead we decided to order through Just Eat. Mum tried the app but slammed her phone onto the table. She wasn't used to ordering on Just Eat. I used my iPhone often to order food, so I took over. Once I had found a carryout we wanted—a Chinese in town—I took voiceover off and handed Mum my phone. This way she could browse through the menu quicker and select what we wanted. Once she'd selected everything, she handed back my phone. Putting my voiceover back on, I completed the purchase. The man who'd shown us to our lodge had said to Dad that if we were ordering in, he had to go up to the barrier to collect it. It was an excuse for Dad to take Dobby out.

Once we'd eaten, we had another soak in the tub. Again, Dad helped me in. I still wasn't ruling out getting one in the future but would have to learn how to get in and out on my own. I was also drinking less now I had Dobby.

To save having another restless night, Dad slept in my room in the other single bed. Dobby lay behind his legs. The only thing was, because Dad was in my room again, I barely got any sleep at all. However, Dobby was happy and that's all that mattered.

Dad had already given Dobby his food, taken him for his walk and started the breakfast before I got up. And once I shuffled through, Dad had bad news.

'There was blood in Dobby's poop this morning,' he announced, as he boiled the eggs.

I sank into the couch. My head was swimming.

'Okay, I'll phone the vet and see what they say' I said, staring across the coffee table.

'I think that's a good idea,' he replied, plating up the breakfast, while Mum made the cups of tea.

Zoe answered and I explained to her that there was no

change with Dobby and there was now blood in his poop. It was Zoe Dad had dealt with on the morning before we left. She suggested I take him to a local vet, and she would send over Dobby's medical history. I did as she said. Thank heaven for smartphones. Dad was already on the case, having heard our conversation.

'There's two vet practices in Musselburgh,' he said, googling local vets. 'I think I saw this one in the way in,' he said.

'Any of the two will do, Dad.'

'This one has a five-star rating.'

'Okay, give me the number for that one and I'll phone them.'

They picked up on the third ring. I explained Dobby's symptoms and that I'd been in touch with my local vet. She asked me to bring him in for half past ten. I pressed my watch to tell me the time. It was 9:40.

'That's fine,' Dad confirmed.

We pulled up outside the vet's with ten minutes to spare. It was the same one Dad had seen on the way in. A few dogs and their owners stood outside. Protocols still didn't allow you to enter the building, and you had to be either seen outside or hand your dog over and they would take him in. However, because I had crutches, a nice female vet made allowances for us. She'd already requested Dobby's notes from my local vet. She took him through to the consultation room while Dad and I waited. I sat biting my nails, Dad's hand on my shoulder.

'He'll be okay,' he said.

'I hope so.' I was holding back tears.

'Okay,' the vet began, returning a short while later. 'He's healthy enough, but after excessive diarrhoea, they do tend to get a little blood in their stool,' she explained. 'Because he's on the fifth day of diarrhoea, I'm going to subscribe some antibiotics and put him on *Hills Intense Digestion* for a few days. He should be fine after a few days,' she assured us.

I puffed out my cheeks with relief.

Dad gave Dobby his antibiotics and a small amount of the tinned food when we got back to the lodge.

We didn't want to exert him too much, so we relaxed in the tub and played games in the lodge all day. A game I could play was Monopoly. I couldn't see the amounts on the paper notes, but Mum and Dad helped. I couldn't see the properties around the board, but Mum and Dad helped with that, too. They also moved my counter for me. I knew most of the streets, anyway. I could recall them from memory. I knew Old Kent Road was a brown square. I knew Pall Mall was a pink one, Fleet Street a… etc. I always made sure I sat in front of the yellow and red properties, as they were the ones I liked to own. I was always good at Monopoly and could still play without being able to see. The game could last for hours but we could easily take a break to re-fill our drinks or nip out for a quick cigarette. Mum and Dad gave up smoking in 2006 and 2007 and thought I would be the last one who would smoke. Me too. Dobby clambered up the couch to watch as we played. Or rather, lie on the top of the back rest like he did at home, behind his dad's head. The game took us up to six o'clock and this time, Mum was able to work out how to use Just Eat. She cooked on our last night.

If a town has a harbour, Dad can't go without visiting it—it's in his nature. It's understandable when he was a fisherman for over thirty years, so we visited Fisher-row on the last day. Dad got my wheelchair out and wheeled me along the promenade. It got us out of the lodge for a bit and also gave Dobby a short walk. There was a slight improvement with Dobby's poops, but not much. He was getting there at least. Mum walked in front with Dobby while Dad pushed me, stopping now and again to look at boats. He liked to check out different yachts; despite owning one himself, he loved to look at others.

Once we were back in the car, I asked Dad to find somewhere to have a cone. You don't go to Musselburgh without getting an ice cream from Scotland's world-renowned ice cream parlour. Mum had a banana one, Dad had his usual raspberry ripple, and I opted for my favourite—mint choc chip. I could see why Luca's were famous for their cones. A lot of dog owners give their dog a cone, but I knew dogs were not allowed dairy, so Dobby wasn't getting one from us. It wouldn't be wise to give him one anyway with the state of his stomach.

I packed for home when we got back to the lodge. Because I take longer than everyone else, the more I got ready the better. It meant I had less to do in the morning. Tea was simple on our last night, as Mum put frozen pizza in the oven. And once we'd finished, we had one last time in the tub. My mind hadn't changed. A hot tub was so beneficial for my breathing, muscles and joints. Some day, in the future, I might still get a hot tub.

Mum had also packed the night before so there was less to do in the morning and Dad began to put things in the car. Scrambled eggs and toast were on the menu before we left, which Mum cooked this time.

Dobby was finally getting better after his week away. If Dobby wasn't better by training on the Wednesday, I wasn't taking him.

<div align="center">~~~</div>

I finally got my new garden shed in October and it arrived the day before I was due to take Dobby back to training. The two men who came to put it up had delivered it in sections and it had already been treated. They asked if I wanted it in the same place. I asked if it could be put a foot closer than the last one because, where it was before, had about a foot's gap between next door's house and the side of my shed. I wanted to close the gap.

They obliged and erected my new shed in no time at all. I could now put my wheelchair back along with other useless things I would probably never use. It was handy to keep bottles of prosecco and crates of juice. I was anxious to know how Dobby would feel with the new shed and if he would try to break it apart like the last one. But he was over a year old now and didn't touch it.

Dobby was better, so he was able to complete his silver award. He passed, but the only way he did was by watching what other dogs were doing. Clever boy. I still wasn't happy though. The silver certificate had my name on it, but I felt that my name should have been left off, as Mum or Dad carried out too much of the training instead of me. I, and I alone, had to complete his gold award. The next block, however, was moving to a Friday, and a later time, which Mum wasn't keen on. And because autumn was looming and the shorter nights were coming in, she didn't want to come out then. I broke the news to Fiona that we were going to leave the gold award until a later date. It wasn't all about the certificates, it was to be able to train my own dog.

Chapter 23

THE SECOND WAVE

Scottish Football Championship, leagues one and two, re-commenced in October, but all fixtures were played behind closed doors. East Fife TV began streaming live matches and season ticket holders could watch the games with an add-on subscription. We were season ticket holders so could log in and watch the games at home. I was unable to cast the live matches to my telly, so I bought a device to link my iPad up and get a full picture.

Mum and Dad watched alternative games at my house and the other at theirs. We treated it like we were at the game by getting pies from the supermarket and heating them up. Dobby was in his element with this arrangement because he was getting attention every week.

At intervals, we had to keep him happy. He dropped a tennis ball at his grandad's feet. He backed away. Growling at his grandad for not throwing it, he moved towards the ball and backed away again. Not pleased, Dobby barked at him. Grandad throwing the ball into the kitchen. Dobby pelted after it and brought it back. Dropping the ball again, Grandad repeated the game. Dobby tried his dad when Grandad had enough. I lay on the living room floor, teased him with the ball before chucking it into the kitchen.

I remembered advice about play time, so, when we all had enough, I raised my hand and said, 'That's enough play,' and he dropped the ball. Although he was toilet trained, he got so excited he sometimes forgot to go outside for a pee. We looked online for away teams' live coverage and paid to watch away games too. So, we watched almost every game.

~~~

The RNIB wanted to keep everyone occupied and active during the long autumn months, so created StepVember—a walking challenge for blind and partially sighted members across Scotland during November. It was never intended as a competition, but everyone wanted to win.

Those who signed up were organised into groups of six. Margaret, my Community Connection Co-ordinator, thought it would be a good idea for me to take part, as I would get out walking with Dobby. StepVember would be a big challenge for me because, although it would have been an excuse to walk Dobby every day, I wouldn't be able to take him every-where with me. However, it was a good way of keeping fit, so I signed up.

~~~

I still had concerns with Dobby's stool in early to mid-No-vember. He was either not touching his kibble or still having the occasional soft poops. After consulting with the vet, he suggested switching to Chappie and monitoring his faecal output. Dobby was lacking fibre in his diet, and he believed this was why Dobby's poops were often soft. Dobby's general health exam was unremarkable, and his dental health was good.

Mum picked up a case of Chappy from the supermarket and I portioned some for his tea. I persisted in giving him his Wainwright's kibble with his Chappy. He ate the lot. A few days later, his poops were like iron. We'd finally cracked it.

News broke on the telly of a Covid vaccination. Pfizer Biontech announced the vaccine everyone had hoped for. I remember watching the German professor when he broke the news on national television.

Just as well because we were entering a second wave. It would take some time for the vaccine roll out, but there was hope for us yet. People were sceptical. Some were conspiracy theorists. Generally, it took years to develop a cure, so people were right to be sceptical. However, if it saved lives, I was taking the vaccine when offered it.

My brother and I stood in my garden. He often popped up to see Dobby. But there was often an ulterior motive to why Uncle Weh dropped in.

'You've heard the news about the vaccine then?' I asked.

'Aye, I have,' he answered, having lit a cigarette.

'I don't suppose you'll be getting the vaccine?'

'No, I won't,' he said, kicking the ball for Dobby to chase.

'I thought as much.'

Dobby was back at his Uncle Weh's feet, waiting for another shot.

'The virus was deliberately made,' he began.

'I'm not disagreeing, Michael. I have my opinions on that as well.'

'Aye, but I read something about the vaccines,' he continued. 'Like the virus, the vaccine was developed to control the population.'

'How d'you figure that one out?' I pondered, Dobby growling at Weh because he hadn't kicked the ball yet.

'I read somewhere that the vaccine makes people infertile.'

'Rubbish,' I replied, taking a puff.

'Believe what you want, Billy, but I'll not be getting the jab,' he insisted, pelting the ball around the garden for Dobby.

'That's your opinion though, Michael. Everyone has a choice. You have to think about Dad and me.'

'What about you and Dad?'

'The virus is more likely to affect us if we catch it.'

'Bullshit.'

'You have to think of the bigger picture. It's a virus which attacks the respiratory system. And Dad and I don't have good respiratory systems.'

'Dad's a fit man,' he stated.

'Aye, I know, but he has COPD!'

'Well, I don't believe in it.' He crushed out his cigarette.

I handed him my one to put out too before countering, 'We'll still be getting our vaccinations.'

It was getting cold standing outside, so once Michael had left, Dobby and I continued with the ball inside where it was warm.

~~~
~~~

StepVember was going well, but I left Dobby at home most times I went for my walk. I obviously took him around the routes we were used to walking together and sometimes I walked him a little further. But leaving him for a while most days was allowing him to get used to being on his own when I went out. StepVember was allowing Dobby not to get separation anxiety.

Besides, I was walking to places in Anstruther I hadn't been in a long time. This was difficult because I couldn't see where I was going. But I knew Anstruther from memory, and although I was a little slow, I got there.

I was determined to walk a few hundred steps a day and sometimes I walked a few thousand steps, but I didn't want to tire myself out and I had my boots to think about. My knees turn inwards when I walk, which means that my ankles also turn inwards.

The NHS have always provided me with custom made footwear. Boots with a raised instep and callipers help to raise my instep, but I have always scraped my toes along the ground, therefore my soles wear down quickly. The more frequently I walked, the quicker my boots needed to be repaired.

I send them to the hospital for repair, but it usually takes three weeks to get them back. I have two pairs, but the rate I was going through them from walking so much, both pairs would need to be repaired.

Covid slowed everything down, which included my boot repair, so for quickness and easiness, Mum took them to Timpsons in St Andrews to be re-soled. It cost me to do this, but it was the only way I would get through StepVember.

Mum, Dad and I sat around the kitchen table as usual on a Friday night, as we had done so often when I talked about getting a dog. This conversation was different. I had Dobby now and we were discussing holidays.

'I don't think we'll be abroad again,' Mum stated, as she took a sip of her wine.

'You never know. I take it Nashville's out then?' I said.

Dad's vodka and coke almost touched his lips when he put it down again, the ice chinking in his glass.

They had intended to take me to Nashville for my fortieth. It was over a year away but would need a lot of planning. It was a lifelong ambition to visit the home of country music. Dad had looked into it before Covid struck and was advised to go in late spring. Country music wasn't their cup of tea, but they were considering going for my benefit.

When most people hear the words country music, they automatically think of Dolly Parton, Glen Campbell, Tammy Wynette and Willie Nelson. Country music isn't all about the classic oldies, there are a lot of talented younger country singers such as Carrie Underwood, Chris Stapleton, Kacey Musgraves. And Kenny Chesney. Even Taylor Swift started out as a country singer. I am a Johnny Cash fanatic, so it would be great to visit the Johnny Cash Museum as well as The Grand Ole Opry.

'We won't be going now,' Dad said, as I imagined him picking at his moustache.

'What, like ever?'

'We don't know how long this virus will be along for, or if it goes away at all,' he said. 'Anyway, your holidays abroad are over.'

'You can't say that, Wullie.'

'I'm being realistic, Joanna,' he said.

'He might,' she offered.

My eyes widened and my jaw dropped when Dad turned his attention to me.

'You wanted a dog!' he retaliated.

'Aye, but he'll be older by then. I'll put him to someone,' I said, my chin quivering.

'Who will you put him to?'

'I'm sure somebody will be happy to take him, Wullie,' Mum said, her bright red lips in that winning smile again. 'I can think of a few who would happily look after him.'

'Sorry, son, it's a long way off yet. Now's not the time.'

'Once people start getting vaccinated, people will be able to travel again,' I pleaded.

'Okay, I'll think about it, but now's not the time,' he said, lifting his glass again.

It was coming to the end of StepVember and I'd gone through two pairs of boots. The man at Timpsons thought the first repair would last, but it didn't. It cost me £70 to get them repaired. I forwarded the receipts to the hospital and was refunded. I was determined to reach ten thousand steps in one day and, although it wasn't a competition, I wanted to achieve my goal.

In order to do this, I had to walk to the edge of Anstruther, find my way to the fire station—near where I used to stay—reach the main road and walk along by the top of Bankie Park. Once I reached St Ayles Church, I crossed the road, along Farm Road, in front of where my old high school used to be, along Dreelside Industrial Estate, down the side of Dreelside where I walk Dobby until I reached home. I checked my health app on my phone and discovered I had walked nearly eleven thousand steps. I was glad it was over, because, although I enjoyed walking, it was too much. And the setting sun disrupted my progress, as sometimes it shone directly in my eyes.

The best feeling about the StepVember challenge was going home to Dobby. Dobby often sat on the kitchen seat waiting for his dad. When he hears the gate open, he jumps onto the kitchen seat, leans on his hind legs, lifts his front paws in the air, letting them hang, and looks through the window like a Meerkat. I enjoy nothing better than roughing his thick hairy coat and allowing him to lick his dad's face when I get home.

Eventually, the Scottish and UK governments eased lockdown restrictions, allowing family bubbles, up to three households and no more than eight family members to get together on Christmas Day. This was okay for us because Michael currently stayed with Mum and Dad, and I was part of their support bubble.

The government anticipated Covid cases would rise but wanted people to enjoy Christmas. Mum and Dad gave their usual trip to Aberdeen a miss, which meant I wouldn't be alone with Dobby over a weekend—although a whole year had passed, and Dobby and I would have been fine if they had. Dad assembled my Christmas tree again, and this time, Dobby had no interest in it. He was such a good boy, and all of his training was paying off. He had stopped chewing and was leaving things alone. Perhaps, when the longer days arrived, I could put him through his gold training and would be proud to have my name on the certificate.

Dad performed the usual routine on Christmas Eve and Christmas Day. But this time he left my presents on my settee. I was confident Dobby wouldn't touch them. And he didn't. Once again, I was able to open them on Christmas morning at home. He was curious but sat in front of me while I tore open the parcels like an over aged, excited child. I knew roughly what I was getting because Mum always asks what I want.

Approaching thirty-nine, I didn't need anything apart from my novelty slippers which I get every year because, like my boots, I go through them quickly. I often get new Blu-ray films to add to my ever-growing collection, which has to number over five hundred by now. New tracksuit bottoms and a sweatshirt are always welcome. I was glad I got new sweatshirts because Dobby chewed holes in the sleeves of my old ones, using them as a tuggy toy. Dobby's presents waited at his granny and grandad's for him.

Dad picked us up as normal and took us down the road. Dobby's present from his granny and grandad was another JML Direct toy, this time a round wooden thing which made a strange noise as it rolled. He got one from me, too, which he chased around the house, dribbling it with his paws.

It was only Mum, Dad, Michael and me for Christmas dinner—and Dobby of course. I allowed Mum to put some peas in with Dobby's food, along with a small piece of turkey, something I was dead against because I was strict on what he got and what people were allowed to give him. But it was

Christmas…

Dobby had been on his walk with his grandad in the morning, but Uncle Weh took him out during the day. He took him along Billow Ness and for a run on the putting green. Michael stopped to chat to a friend and when he turned around, he saw a fleck of white disappearing into the distance. He wasn't long in coming back when his Uncle Weh roared after him. He made a slow retreat—his tail down and ears drooping; the signs he knows he's done something wrong.

For a few weeks, we thought Michael was keeping something from us. And on Christmas night, he came clean. He'd been seeing someone.

'D'you think it's a good idea seeing someone?' I asked, joining him outside for a cigarette.

'What d'you mean?'

'We're advised to avoid starting a relationship with someone new because the virus is so high.'

'I don't believe in the virus,' he said, his mind clearly not changed.

'I know how you feel, Michael, but you still have to think about your family! Dad has COPD,' I reminded him. 'And you have a son with severe asthma.'

'Ah, but there's nothing wrong with them,' he insisted. 'They're healthy people.'

'A lot of healthy people have died from Covid. I heard a woman returned home from Ibiza, tested positive for Covid, visited her boyfriend, he caught the virus from her, showed no symptoms, passed it onto his dad and his dad died.'

'Really?' he asked.

'Aye, really.'

Dad passed us a few times, taking things to the bins, probably trying to catch what we were talking about.

'But it's up to you, Michael,' I added.

We usually play games as a family and carry on having a few drinks after our meal, but Michael left for the night, and I wanted to spend Christmas night at home with Dobby. If I stayed to socialise, I would just have one drink after another and struggle home. So, Dad walked Dobby and me up the road. I could have more drinks at home with Dobby cuddled up beside me on the couch.

We had no football to watch at the start of 2021 because Scottish leagues one and two were suspended again from the 2nd of January. Unless you had Sky Sports or TNT Sports, which fortunately I did, then there were plenty of Arsenal and Celtic matches to watch. We just had to wait for our division to re-commence, if it ever did.

Chapter 24

BANG OUT OF ORDER

Storm Darcy battered Britain in early February 2021, which meant my walks with Dobby were limited and Mum and Dad had to walk him for me. In comparison to the previous year before the pandemic, the early part of 2021 was bitterly cold. Dobby and I were at Mum and Dad's for tea when the wind began to strengthen. A storm is usually on the way when a day or two before it arrives, there is no wind. But Darcy arrived with vengeance.

'I'm not sure if you should be down here tonight,' Mum said, watching the latest developments on the news.

'I should be fine,' I replied. 'The wind's not too bad.'

However, while I sat, I listened to the wind rise.

'I think I'll ask your dad to nip you both up the road when he gets home.'

'I think that'll actually be a wise move,' I agreed.

The storm was still tame when Dad wheeled me home, Dobby walking by my wheelchair. But Mum had made the right decision because a couple of hours later, the storm raged. Garden fences groaned in protest. I heard a few crash-es during the night and wondered if my fence had fallen to the ground. It had done once before when a previous storm reached eighty miles per hour, and it took some convincing for the council to give me a new one. Without a fence, my garden is totally exposed. Dobby's head popped up now and again when he heard another gust blowing a wheely bin down. The storm was clearly upsetting him, but there was nothing we could do apart from wait it out.

My fence was still intact, which was a relief because how would I keep Dobby in if it had blown down? The fence which enclosed the electrical boxes across the road wasn't as fortunate. And to my amazement, when Dad came to walk Dobby in the morning, he told me half of my neighbour's wall had blown down.

Darcy subsided but it was replaced by snow. I did say we rarely see snow, with us being so close to the sea, but when it arrives from the east, we tend to get it bad. Nothing could be worse than the Beast from the East in 2018, but as much as thirty centimetres fell in some parts of the UK. There wasn't as much in Anstruther, but enough to keep me indoors for a while longer.

I didn't know how Dobby would cope with snow, as he had never seen it before. He loved it. It was a new feeling on his paws. Mum and Dad had difficulty walking him. He just wanted to roll in the stuff. I, on the other hand found the snow an annoyance. Dobby's a white dog. I couldn't see him when I let him out. And I couldn't get him inside. It was worse when the snow turned to ice a few days later.

Fourteen months had passed since Dobby stopped peeing in the house. It was difficult to know if Dobby needed to go.

The only way I learned he was desperate for the toilet was if he walked to the door, came back to me and walked to the door again. He didn't even bark or scratch a paw against the door. Another way he let me know he needed to go was if he lay on the mat. However, one night he woke me three times. I thought he needed out, but he *wanted* out. I sat to have a cigarette each time he did. I heard strange crunching noises. He had grown out of chewing things, but this sound was different. All the little bugger wanted was to eat the ice. He got his dad out of bed for that! I was glad when the snow and ice melted. At least I got a decent night's sleep.

~~~

By early March, the weather had improved, and I was able to walk Dobby again. Time had passed and despite having told everyone to keep Dobby on the lead, I was now walking him off the lead. I felt comfortable as long as someone was with me. This was usually Mum. His lead was attached to my belt until we reached the park. I unclipped it when we got to the cycle path.

However, unclipping his lead wasn't easy. Every time I approached him, he backed away. I tried again and the same happened. I soon realised the problem. He's never liked my crutches. He's okay walking beside me, but if the crutches get too close, he jumps out of the way.

He had had an incident with the crutches when he was a puppy. Uncle Weh was playing with him when my crutches fell on him. He's been scared of them since, despite my saying, 'They won't hurt you, Dobby.' Once I had managed to unclip
~~~

the lead, I gave him a treat and he was fine. I tried to keep Dobby close while Mum and I walked along the cycle path, but he was busy investigating. We called him to us, but he would wander off into the undergrowth again. He enjoyed running through the leaves. I didn't. I tried to stop Dad letting him forage through them. Anything could have been hidden in the pile of leaves, but he liked the sensation on his legs and paws. He was still bad for running to see other dogs, but he was only saying hello and would soon come back to us. If he didn't, we kept walking, and he wasn't long in catching up.

We don't re-attach his lead when we reach the car park because we know how streetwise he is, due to the excessive training we've put him through. He doesn't need his lead on to go back to the house. He doesn't need it on to go to the park either, but I prefer to put it on. It started to rain the closer we got home, and I was desperate for a pee.

'You go ahead with Dobby, Mum and get the door open,' I told her, attempting with great difficulty to hold my bladder.

'Okay,' she said, hurrying off.

I'd only reached my row of houses when Dobby appeared in front of me. Mum had gone ahead, but Dobby came back to see where his dad was. Once he reached me, he turned around and walked behind me back to the house. If he could do that, I could surely walk him off the lead on my own.

Things changed dramatically two days later. After tea at Mum and Dad's on the Sunday, I walked home as normal. Dad and Dobby went in the opposite direction. He planned to walk Dobby along Billow Ness and finish with a runabout on the putting green. Dad arrived back with Dobby sooner than

I expected. Dobby couldn't get in the door quickly enough. He found me, hid behind me and his little body trembled against my legs. I reached down to stroke his belly, and his heart pounded against my hand.

'Some idiot let off a firework on the putting green,' Dad announced, removing Dobby's collar.

'You're fucking joking! That's bang out of order. Do you know who it was?'

'I'm not sure. I don't think he knew where he was or which planet he was on. I just know he had Rangers gear on.'

Rangers won the Scottish Premiership earlier that day. It was the first time they'd won the league in ten years. I was disappointed Celtic didn't win, and I had nothing against Rangers, despite the rivalry between the two clubs.

'Did you not have a word with him?'

'No, he was out of his nut. It probably wouldn't have made a difference, anyway.'

'Dobby's usually okay with fireworks.' I was trying to calm him down with gentle strokes to his belly, back and head.

'Aye, but the guy set it off right next to him. It scared the life out of him. He more or less pulled me up the road.'

'He'll remember that for the rest of his days.'

'Aye, I know. If I had seen the guy, I wouldn't have taken Dobby to the putting green.'

'It's not your fault, Dad. You weren't to know he was going to let a firework off.'

I had an idea who the man might have been, but I never found out. I put a message on Facebook explaining what happened and hoped someone would come forward with an apology at least. No one did. Some people just don't think and don't realise how it impacts pets and their owners. I swore if I ever found out who set off the firework, I would wring his neck. But wringing his neck wouldn't achieve anything. I had a dog who would probably be terrified for the rest of his life. I monitored Dobby for a few days to see if he got it out of his system. He didn't. He was wary of every bang he heard.

Chapter 25

PERSEVERANCE

It was mid to late March before it got a little bit warmer. We took Dobby to West Sands in St Andrews. I said I would never manage a beach with Dobby, but it didn't have to be the beach. There is still a lovely walk along by the golf course. This was too far for me, so we took my wheelchair.

Dad pulled the van into the car park. They had a second van now that Mum was helping Dad out with the fish round, and we used it more. It also had more room in the middle for transporting the wheelchair. I still felt the cold when I opened the van door. At least it wasn't windy, and it was dry. Dad positioned the chair at the door, and I slid myself in. I couldn't keep warm sitting in a chair, but Mum and Dad could by walking. We began our journey. This was also a test to see if Dobby could walk off his lead. I still wasn't keen on this, especially in a different place. We kept him on his lead for the first part of his walk, while Dad pushed me. Dad has always walked at a quick pace and Mum struggled to keep up.

Dobby wasn't sure of the wheelchair to begin with when he was little. He must have thought the chair was a threat like my crutches. He often got a ride on my lap when he was a puppy, but walking beside the chair was a different story. He didn't know what to do and if the wheels got too close, he jumped out of the way. He yelped once when the front of the chair caught his paw. All of that changed! It took a little work, but he learned to walk on the left-hand side of the wheelchair. When it's just Dobby, Dad and me, I hold Dobby's lead, and he happily trots alongside the chair. Mum took Dobby this time and they both walked on the left.

Dobby hasn't really pulled and he has adapted to different people's paces. However, I was horrified when I listened to Dobby walk alongside me. Dad continued to walk fast, Mum tried to keep up and I heard Dobby choke. His collar pressed on his Adam's apple as he strained to keep up.

'Would you slow down, Dad?'

'Aye, Wullie, you are going a bit fast.'

'Sorry,' he said, slowing down a bit.

'We're not in any hurry,' I added.

Dad probably wouldn't have been aware of Dobby choking. Dad is quite deaf in one ear and was focused on the path ahead. But if Dobby choked with his lead pulling on his collar, I had to do something about it.

We walked for a couple of miles around the golf course before we turned around and headed back, with me reminding Dad to slow down.

'Okay, you can unclip the lead now.' I was, satisfied that Dobby wouldn't be in any danger.

'It's about time,' Dad said, stopping to allow Mum to unclip his lead. 'He's good off his lead,' he added.

'I've no doubt he is, Dad.'

I've always known my dog would be capable of walking off his lead, but I tried to convey the message that everyone had to follow my instructions and only do things when I wanted.

Dobby did walk beside us but had a tendency to stray slightly to investigate a smell—the reason I preferred to have him close. He was a good dog and when he wandered too far, one of us called him and he came to us. I wish he followed the same command during training. The three of us froze when we heard a golfer tee-off towards the eighteenth hole. Dobby's ears pricked up on hearing the sound. Dobby ran off when he heard someone tee-off at Anstruther. He loved to chase after the player's golf ball. He was poised to do the same at The Old Course.

'Dobby,' Mum warned.

He looked at his granny and looked back in the direction of the ball.

'Dobby,' don't you dare,' I threatened.

His grandad raised a hand, Dobby turned around and continued walking.

'Good boy,' I said, and Mum rewarded him with a treat.

I still didn't want my dog to wear a harness. Dobby had been brought up wearing a collar, and it didn't bother him. He wasn't comfortable with something wrapped around his body and I didn't like to smother him by putting one on him. He wouldn't budge with one on anyway. But I wasn't letting him choke, so I looked on Amazon a few days later for a harness. Trying him with one again wouldn't hurt. A lot of dog owners prefer a *Julius-K9 power harness*. I didn't know what kind of harness this was, but a friend recommended one and said they were easy to use. I couldn't find one in the colour I wanted for a small breed. They sold black ones, red ones and green was a popular colour. But no white ones. I chose the lime green one.

I had been back in touch with a friend I met when I studied at Glenrothes college between 2000 and 2002. Like the other friends I met at the same time, we went our separate ways. I still keep in touch with some of them and learned that Yvonne was selling off old stock from when she was Body Shop ambassador. She had some items I wanted. We began talking more again and video called each other. She owned a seven-year-old Border terrier called Zack. She could have posted me the items, but it was a good excuse to bring them along and have a catch-up. Dobby and Zack would also get a play with each other.

A few days later, Yvonne made arrangements to come along one Saturday at the end of March. She tested regularly to make sure she had no symptoms before coming along. She was clear. Yvonne aimed to arrive mid-morning.

Dobby's new Julius K-9 arrived earlier that day and Dad removed it from the packaging. He examined it and worked out how to put it on Dobby. I hoped he would show me, but he placed it on the kitchen table. He said he had things to do and would show me later and stepped outside. As he done so, I heard a car pull up and I also stepped outside.

Yvonne called to us when she opened her car door.

'Who's that?' Dad asked, approaching the gate.

'That's Yvonne, my old friend from college,' I replied.

'Oh aye, I remember her,' he said.

It had been twenty years since Dad had last seen Yvonne, so I was surprised he recognised her.

Dad left us to catch up. I wrestled with the bolt on the shed door to get chairs out. It was stiff and took a lot of wiggling.

'I'll get that,' Yvonne said, taking over.

'Okay.' I stood back.

'You have prosecco!' she said, removing two chairs.

'I do,' I replied. 'D'you want some?'

'Not just now,' she said, laughing as she brought the chairs out and closed the door.

She placed the chairs a couple of metres apart. Yvonne was still Covid-cautious, so she felt safer sitting outside. She put my bag of goodies on the table before sitting down.

Dobby and Zack hit it off immediately. They chased each other around the garden. In and out of the house. They repeated this for a while until Dobby got fed up and lay beside me. It's usually Dobby who is desperate to play. Zack and Dobby were similar in size. They are both terriers and have the same traits. But Zack is a Border terrier—a dog I did consider getting before I settled on a Jack Russell. Zack had longer legs, standing a little taller than Dobby. They had the same ears. Zack growled with a ball in his mouth.

'He's wanting to play,' Yvonne said.

'Aye, Dobby's the same. He often growls with the ball in front of him or lies with it under his chin.'

It had been so long since Yvonne and I had seen one another, but she hadn't changed a bit. She was the same bubbly person I met at college. She had the same, sweet laugh that you just want to cuddle. The same long brunette hair which cascaded down her back. And the same winning smile I adored when I first met her when I still had some sight. We sat and talked about everything from college to what she was up to after she and her husband had split up.

I wanted to know how the harness worked and didn't want to wait for Dad, so I fetched it from the kitchen table and brought it outside. I rolled the harness around in my hands as Yvonne spoke, wondering how to ask for her help.

'Would you like a hand with that?' she asked, noticing my confused expression.

'Aye, that'll be good Yvonne, thanks.'

'Hold the harness like this,' she instructed, placing it in my hands. 'His head goes through the loop at the front of the harness.'

'Right, okay.'

'Take that strap and find the clip on the left.'

'Okay, got it,' I said.

'That strap goes under his belly, and you clip it in.'

'That's it?' I asked, surprised how easy it was.

'Yeah, that's it.'

'I suppose I'd better try it on him then,' I said.

Yvonne picked Dobby up and placed him on my lap. I put his head through the loop and put the strap under his belly like she said and clipped it in.

It was simple. I could put it on him hassle free. But when I lowered him on the ground, he wouldn't move. It was just like before. I remember trying him with a harness before in the house. He lay on the pouffe and wouldn't move. He lay across his dad, expecting me to take it off. I had been too soft then, but I had to persevere this time.

'What a handsome wee man you are,' Yvonne said, sitting back down, hearing her little chuckle as she did so.

'I'm not sure how long that'll last, Yvonne. We tried him with a harness when he was little, but he didn't budge then.'

'Just stick with it and he'll learn.'

'I hope you're right. I need him to wear it because his collar chokes him when his lead is attached.'

'I've never used a harness.'

'You haven't?'

'No, he doesn't need one.'

'Well, I wasn't keen either, but Dobby's going to learn to wear a harness if he likes it or not!'

However, I didn't want to punish him by leaving it on him. I took it off and promised I would put it on and take it off intermittently. Hopefully, he would get used to wearing it that way.

I was conscious of the time. East Fife were playing that day, and it was Mum and Dad's turn to host. I thought I was going to have to give it a miss if Yvonne stayed much longer.

'I'll better get going,' she announced.

'I'm sorry I couldn't offer you anything to eat. If I'd planned things better, we could have gone for lunch or something.'

'That's okay. Don't worry about it. I can come along again, and we can go for a chippy or something,' she went on. 'We can take the dogs along Elie beach.'

I didn't like to say I couldn't walk on a beach, but agreed, and offered a small smile.

'That'll be good, Yvonne.'

'You have prosecco in your shed. I can come along and have a drink with you.'

'I would like that, too.'

'Have you ever tried gin with prosecco?' she asked, packing up her things.

'No, I've not.'

'Oh well, you'll have to try it.'

'You and Zack can stay when you come for a drink!'

'Thanks for the offer, but I've got a persuasive Dad who will come for me.'

'Okay, no problem,' I said.

'C'mon then Zack.' She encouraged him to the gate.

'Thanks for the visit,' I said, before she left.

'No problem. I'll be in touch.'

I watched them both get back in the car and hoped she was true to her word as the car backed up before driving away.

Dad started to try Dobby with his harness, but as I expected, he wouldn't move.

'Keep persevering, Dad, and he'll learn it has to go on him.'

Dad did persevere, but it was no good. Dobby was very stubborn. If Dobby didn't walk with it on, Dad took it off and put it back on further along. I remember him telling me, 'I put it on him at the start of the park and I began walking. Thinking he would begin to follow me, I continued walking. I looked back and he was still sitting in the same spot. I saw this little white speck the further away I got.'

'Did he still not move?'

'No, I had to walk back.'

'Keep persevering,' I said.

I also continued putting it on and taking it off in the house and in the garden. This wasn't easy—especially in the garden because I couldn't find him. He often hid somewhere when he saw the harness—most likely behind the wall. I looked everywhere for him. If he was in the house and saw the harness in my hand, he walked away. If he was on the couch when I approached him, he jumped down and moved away. It was easier if he headed to the back door or went into the bedroom. He usually lay down in a corner, which made it easier to slip it on him. Mum didn't find it easy either, but at least she could see where he was. We both began saying, 'Don't walk away from me,' lyrics from a Whitney Houston song. But unlike before when he came to you to put his collar on, he refused with the harness. Once on, he shook his body as if thinking, 'If I shake this thing, it might fall off.' No such luck.

Eventually, however, if I left it on, he did start to walk around the house and in the garden with it on. He still hated it but began walking outside with it on. And by the middle of April, he began to wear the harness to go for his walks whether it be with his grandad, granny or his dad. We'd all been too soft with him and should have persevered when he was younger, but I wasn't giving in this time. And the more we persisted, the more it paid off.

Chapter 26

THE DOG SCARER

The weather warmed up. Dad was quiet workwise at the weekends, so we took a drive to walk Dobby in different places. We debated whether to go to Lochore Meadows in Lochgelly or Loch Leven in Kinross—both places I'd been to with my blind group, BASE. On this occasion we chose Loch Leven. Mum made sandwiches and we took Dobby's food with us. Dobby got fed up with his Chappy, so again, we had to mix things up to encourage him to eat his food.

I remember when BASE took a trip to one of the islands. Two boats took us across to Loch Leven Castle. The island on which the castle was situated was difficult for my wheelchair and the volunteer pushing me. It was hilly and grassy—quite deep for my wheels to go through. The party knew I could get out and use my crutches, but several of them persisted by helping to push the chair.

It was interesting to hear the tour guides explain about how Mary Queen of Scots first visited the castle in 1561 and was held prisoner between 1567/1568. She miscarried a baby to her third husband, the Earl of Bothwell and escaped across the loch in 1568. She was in exile in England and never returned to Scotland.

Part of what I enjoy about BASE events is the lunch afterwards. Lunch often consists of soup, sandwiches, tea and coffee. Volunteers of BASE always make sure I am stocked up on plenty of sandwiches. Despite me saying I am full, they keep on loading my plate.

There were lots of people relaxing on the outside seating area when we pulled into the car park. People had only just started getting out again after the latest restrictions had lifted. The café where BASE had lunch was closed. You could still buy a tea or coffee to take away, so people sat on picnic benches with their family and dogs drinking hot beverages. The place was mobbed. I enjoy a coffee when I am out, but I decided to leave it this time and ask Mum and Dad when we returned from our walk, providing it wasn't as busy.

Dad got my wheelchair out of the boot and assembled the power pack. My wheelchairs have never been manual ones because I can't see to steer them. Nor have they been electric powered for the same reason. However, in recent years, Dad has found it more difficult to push me—especially up hills. To make it easier on Dad, I arranged for my chair to be adapted so you can fit a power pack. This aided Dad, making it easier to push my chair. He often forgot to lift the key before leaving home but remembered this time. Just as well! Some areas were more difficult to negotiate than others. It was better once we were on the gravel path, but even this was problematic.

Dobby positioned himself next to the chair, on the left hand-side, where his granny walked with him. Dobby, at times, didn't seem to know the harness was on him the way he trotted along. Every so often, he and his granny walked ahead, leaving Dad to navigate the twigs and tree roots. If they wandered too far ahead, Dobby stopped, looked back and waited on us to catch up.

We found a bench a mile or so into our walk so stopped for our sandwiches. Dad put Dobby's food down for him, but he didn't touch it. After lunch, we continued, avoiding people coming towards us and stepping aside to let people on bikes past.

It was time to turn around after three-and-a-half miles, as the more we walked, the further back it was. It's about thirteen miles around the loch, so Dobby would have walked seven of those thirteen miles—plenty for him, although he is capable of walking the full distance.

I asked Mum to unclip Dobby's lead because the woodland track was far enough from the water's edge—not that he would go in. Dobby walked all the way back without his lead. When we reached the car park, the picnic area was busier than before. I asked Mum and Dad if I could have a take-out coffee, and they obliged. I allowed Dobby to play with other dogs before we returned to the car and headed home. Dobby flaked out on the couch when we got back.

~~~

Dad erected my gazebo in April. He thought it would be better putting it up earlier on in the year. Dobby was content lying in the garden. April was fairly warm, so if Dobby was happy, so was I. Allowing Dobby to sun himself or shelter
~~~

under the gazebo meant that he wouldn't come inside for his tea. I placed tubs of water outside for him, but he didn't touch them. And more often than not, I couldn't get him in the house at night. The cheese trick worked only for so long. As soon as he heard the fridge door open, he knew what was coming and dashed inside. This stopped after a while, as he became wise to it and stopped coming in for his reward.

I stood beside the doorstep, pointed into the house and called, 'IN!' Occasionally he reacted, but if he did, it was a rarity. I had to walk around the garden looking for him. The gazebo provided an additional hiding place. I started at one end of the wall, slid my bum along, feeling with one hand. I often found him curled up like a ball behind the gazebo flap. I had to scoop him under my arm and carry him to the house.

'What are you doing with the living room door closed?' Dad asked one day when I sat on the doorstep having a cigarette.

'I sometimes can't get him in again if I let him out,' I replied.

'You can't keep him in!'

'I know, Dad, and I don't keep him in.'

Dad stepped past me, opened the living room door and Dobby ran through.

I often sat on the doorstep to have a cigarette when I would hear Dobby behind me. He usually had something in his mouth that he wanted to sneak out with. He took tentative, tiny steps, thinking I wouldn't hear him. I reached my arm behind me, and he backed away. He tried again. It was the same outcome. However, Dobby is very clever and sneaky. If he's determined to achieve something, he will. I wasn't quick enough on Dobby's third attempt. He managed to evade my hand, and I had to feel around for what he had taken outside. I wanted Dad to take the gazebo down again, but he persuaded me to keep it up because it was a good shelter for Dobby.

<div style="text-align:center">~~~</div>

My blue envelope arrived through my letterbox with the date of my Covid vaccination. I knew I was in the vulnerable category but didn't expect my turn as early as April. However, it was news I welcomed. It meant I might live longer and be able to continue raising my dog. The vaccines were being rolled out at the East Neuk Centre—a place I used to know so well. Dad took me for my vaccine, but it was closed. The stock hadn't arrived yet. We were asked to go back late morning. We tried again. This time it was open. The vaccine stations were set up in the big hall where I used to attend youth club with my friends.

'Over here, Billy,' a woman's voice called.

It's usually William, my surname or both when being addressed by a health care professional, but she knew me. I was sure I recognised the voice from somewhere. Dad walked me over and sat me in front of the woman. When she spoke again, I realised who it was—It was one of the volunteers from BASE.

'How are you?' she asked.

'Yeah, I'm fine, thanks.'

She told me which vaccine she was going to administer

and explained some of the symptoms I might experience. But before she inserted the needle into my muscle, she asked if I was allergic to anything.

'Yes, I am,' I said, without any hesitation.

'What are you allergic to?' she asked.

'I don't know. I'm still under investigation to see what causes it.'

'I don't think I can give you this if you have an undiagnosed allergy,' she said. 'You'll have to find out what you're allergic to first.'

'I have angioedema,' I said. 'That means my mouth swells up from time-to-time. It might be an allergy, or it might not.'

'I'll check with my superior to see if I'm able to give you this,' she offered.

'I don't think you're getting this,' Dad said, once she'd gone.

'I don't think so either.'

'Okay,' she began, sitting down again. 'I can't give you this today, but you need it so contact your doctor to hurry along with the investigation.'

I gulped, holding back tears. She was doing the right thing. She didn't want to put something in my arm if it would harm me.

I phoned my doctor the same day to explain why I hadn't got my Covid vaccination. Getting past reception was harder than getting the vaccine itself. After explaining why I needed to see or speak to a doctor, I was finally issued with a time when one would phone me back. My doctor had read my notes prior to calling me back.

'They should have given you that vaccine, William,' she said.

'I know, I tried telling her that. I have angioedema and take medication to control it.'

'That's right, William. I notice you've not been seen by a specialist yet.'

'No, I haven't. It was supposed to be an emergency. That was nearly three years ago.'

I had woken one Saturday morning in June 2018, and I couldn't breathe. The inside of my mouth had swollen up. My cheeks ballooned and my lips were as big as melon slices. I looked like Desperate Dan. The out-of-hours doctor said, 'You've had an allergic reaction to something.' He pumped a load of pills into me to bring the swelling down, but it took two days to subside completely.

'I'll hurry that appointment along for you,' my GP offered.

'That's great, doctor,' I replied. 'What do I do about my vaccination in the meantime?'

'I would phone and get another appointment for the jab because your angioedema has nothing to prevent you from being vaccinated.'

'I thought that,' I said.

I managed to re-book my Covid vaccination and got it ten days later. My friend, Dave told me I would probably be unwell after the jab, and I was. I ached all over and I burned up. Plus, I had a splitting headache. Luckily, I was fine the next day.

~~~
~~~

When Dobby didn't walk away or hide and allowed me to put his harness on, I had an idea. Like before when I first thought I could walk him on my own, it was time I tried him off his lead. He hated getting his harness on and still tried to shake it off, but it didn't bother him once it was on. It couldn't be too difficult for me to walk him off his lead, could it?

Instead of doing it in secret, I told Mum what I was going to do. She was fine with it. I asked her to hang back until Dobby and I had a good start. I had the lead on him until I reached the park as usual and bent down to unclip him once there.

My hand was shaking as if I'd been on a week's drinking bender. I was about to take it to the next level. This was something else Dad said I wouldn't manage, and I never thought I would do, either. I began along the cycle path. My legs were shaking like glass bottles on a shelf which were in danger of falling off during an earthquake. I continued on.

'Come here, Dobby.' I clicked my fingers.

I heard his name tag jangling, and he appeared by my side.

'Good boy,' I said, rewarding him with a treat.

We walked on and he was very good. He stayed with me most of the way. When I thought he had wandered again, I called him to me. He came and earned another treat. We reached the end of the cycle path, onto the other path which led to the car park when I was sure Dobby spotted someone.

'It's no one you know,' I said, not knowing if it was some-one he knew or not.

Lowering myself to a crouching position, I said, rubbing him behind his ears, 'You've been such a good boy for your dad.' We got to the kerb at the end of the path, and I asked him to sit. By this time, I was unsure and wasn't confident enough to continue with him through the car park, so I slid my phone from my pocket and messaged Mum.

'You can catch up now,' I wrote.

Mum arrived in seconds and Dobby bolted back along the path to greet her after hearing her call him.

'I didn't feel comfortable from here,' I said, when she caught up.

'You did well. I watched you both all the way.'

'And he didn't see you?'

'There were a couple of times when I had to slip out of sight, but no, he didn't see me.'

'What about when we turned the corner?'

'That was a close one, but I managed to stay hidden.'

We continued back to the house with Dobby off his lead and I thought if I could do it once, I would be able to walk him off his lead more often. However, I still felt safer keeping him on his lead.

Friends, Mum, Dad and I took Dobby to the park so often now. One of my friends took Dobby and his dog for a run around the park. Dobby ran to a bush and shivered under it.

'I don't know what happened to Dobby,' he said when they returned. 'He started shaking.'

'I don't know why he would do that,' I said. 'Maybe something spooked him.'

'Possibly.'

'It's out of character. He loves the park.'

The next time Mum and I walked Dobby around the park,

my stomach churned. The colour drained from my face. I had heard them so often, but never thought to consider how Dobby would cope.

He didn't react to them before that firework went off on the putting green. Farmers' bird scarers are supposed to keep birds off of their crops and vegetables. Dobby was going to think every bang was a firework. He didn't hide under a bush with us, but his tail dropped, and his ears drooped on hearing the bird scarer. I became vigilant when I heard it and knew this was going to become a big problem—especially on walks. He would think every loud noise was a threat to him. Everywhere he loved to walk changed.

Chapter 27

DOBBY'S SECOND BIRTHDAY

Macar, Jan, Lewis, Claire and I arranged to meet in Edinburgh. This time it was to watch Scotland play against Czech Republic in their opening match in Euro 2020. The European Championships scheduled for 2020 was cancelled due to Covid but was played in 2021 instead. Our small group had been meeting over Zoom regularly over the last few weeks and planned to watch the Scotland match together for the first time.

Scotland's match against the Czech Republic was five days before Dobby's planned party. Mum and Dad drove me to the station, and I checked in to let passenger assist know I'd arrived. Dobby watched with his granny and grandad as the train took me away. Dobby was getting used to me going places and knew I would be coming home again.

I was chewing on my bottom lip the closer I got to Edinburgh, but I was excited to spend the day with my friends and Dobby being occupied with his granny and grandad took my mind off being away from him.

When I got back, he would be waiting for me this time, rather than his granny and grandad keeping him overnight.

Four of us met at Waverley Station to then go to The Tron—a pub not far from the station. It was within walking distance, but Macar wanted to take a taxi, so we piled into the nearest one. Carl's nickname is Macar. He arranged and booked the pub so the five of us could watch the game. Claire's mum and dad drove her through, as they came from Gourock, Inverclyde. Claire and I spoke on the phone a lot, but it was the first time we had met in person.

The positions in which we sat were wrong. Lewis, who had no sight, sat in front of the telly. Macar, who also had no sight, was behind him. Claire sat in between Lewis and Jan. I was stuck on the end and couldn't see the telly. I swapped with Lewis, which meant I had a good view of the game, but it was really an excuse to sit next to Claire.

It was like our group had our own private room upstairs. We were the only ones there. Apparently, downstairs was full. I enjoyed watching the game with my friends, and despite the defeat, we all enjoyed ourselves. Once the game had finished, we walked to the pub next door. I think we had a further two drinks before Jan called me a taxi back to the station. I had a great time, but I didn't want to be late because I had arranged for Dad to pick me up from Leuchars and I wanted to get home to Dobby.

They both stood waiting for me on the platform. Dobby sat on my lap staring out of the window on our way home. We played tuggy for a bit, allowing me to swing him around the living room, his teeth attached to the rope for dear life, not letting go. Fetching a tennis ball, I placed it on the floor. Growling at his dad for not throwing it, I swooped it up, tossed it behind me and he pelted after it. When we'd both had enough, we headed to bed, cuddling up to each other.

With the support of family and friends, I had successfully raised Dobby so far and wanted to celebrate my achievements on his second birthday. I didn't plan on holding a party for him every year, but since government restrictions allowed larger gatherings again, I was able to celebrate his birthday during the month in which he was born.

The weather in June wasn't as warm as the previous year, but it was pleasant. I arranged a butcher's delivery of burgers and sausages to arrive on the Saturday of his party. I had been ordering deliveries from the butchers more often throughout lock-down because steak pie, mince round, sausages and burgers were easy for me to cook. Corned beef slices were also simple to put in a roll. Dobby was always curious when I took my deliveries inside, and he sniffed furiously when I put the bag on the floor to unpack it.

'That's not for you, Dobby' I said, putting away items which went in the fridge and the others in the freezer for later.

I invited most of the same guests as I had in September, including my family, some friends, family friends and the *Dreelside Shenanigans*. There were also new members to the family.

My brother, Uncle Weh, had been seeing his new girlfriend for a few months now. Zuzu was a lovely Slovakian woman with long blonde hair. She had two children of her own, a lot younger than my niece and nephew. Zuzu's children were around ten and eight years old. I wondered how Michael had met this intriguing woman. My mum's auntie lived across the road from me, and I learned that Zuzu visited her regularly because she used to be married to one of my half cousins, and her children were my mum's Auntie Nina's grandchildren. Michael must have seen her going in and out of her house when he came to see Dobby.

When Michael gets a new van, he spends a lot of time converting it into a camper van. Dobby was excited when his Uncle Weh turned up for him. Michael and Zuzu often met at my house to take Dobby and her children for a run along Elie beach. Most weekends, they were away for hours. When Dobby was younger, I didn't like him away from me for more than half-an-hour, but I was okay with him being away for longer now, as he was enjoying himself.

Jack Russells are energetic dogs and will play for hours if you let them, but when they brought Dobby home, he padded to the couch, jumped up and flaked out. This meant I could watch the telly for longer, drinking from my Holy Grail, as Dobby slept soundly beside me. Michael once asked me if he could take Dobby away for a few days, but as much as I would miss him, and knew Dobby and his Uncle Weh would love to travel for a few days, I wasn't ready for that.

~~~

On the day of the party, Mum and Dad arrived before everyone else again to make sure everything was ready for guests to arrive. Lynne brought her gazebo round again, but because the shed was where the gazebo was the last time, it was put up next to my one. Once everything was sorted and ready for the party, Mum and Dad left for a couple of hours.
~~~

I had spent a few weeks, but not months as before, updating Dobby's birthday playlist.

More guests began to arrive including Dobby's friends, the cocker spaniel and the Maltese-chihuahua cross. Dobby was in his element with all of these different people and dogs. The music was playing from my Bluetooth speaker, the afternoon was heating up and so was the barbecue. There were a lot of eager, hungry people, racing to get to the barbecue first for a freshly cooked burger or hot dog. I asked someone to fetch one for me.

Like the previous September, some guests gave titbits to Dobby from their plates, despite knowing he wasn't allowed any. Shaking my head I puffed out my cheeks. I let it go because it was just one day with lots of guests. Fewer guests, and I would have been tougher with the guilty parties. Dobby's bags of kibble still lay against the kitchen wall, but although Dobby never bothered for them, the other dogs did. We had to take the bags away and lift Dobby's untouched breakfast or the other dogs would eat that, too.

The day turned into early evening and early evening turned into night. The majority of guests stayed all day enjoying each other's company, eating lots of food and some encouraged me to do a Johnny Cash song, but I didn't feel like it. Instead, I was happy sitting listening to everyone else enjoying themselves and was glad the day was a success for Dobby's second birthday. When everyone went home, Mum, Dad and I finished off the evening with a nightcap under my gazebo and talked about Dobby.

'It's been a good day,' I said, sipping prosecco from my

Holy Grail.

'Aye, it has,' Dad agreed, with a fresh vodka and coke in his hand.

'Dobby seemed to have a good time,' Mum added.

'Aye, he did,' I said.

'He's a really good dog,' Mum said.

'Aye, he is.' I raised my glass to my lips.

'It's a shame we didn't keep his testicles,' Dad said, looking at Dobby foraging for scraps. 'He would have made a good hunting dog.' He took another sip.

'It had to be done,' I said.

'I know it had to be done,' Dad went on. 'I'm just saying, he would have made a good hunting dog.'

'I didn't get him for hunting, Dad! I got him for a pet.'

'Hunting is in their nature,' he persisted.

'I know, Dad, but he's still a pet,' I said, flailing my arms. 'I take him to training to domesticate him.'

'I have a customer who has Jack Russells and he uses them to get rid of vermin on his farm.'

'That's him though,' I said, smacking my thighs. 'My dog is a pet, and I've trained him to be a pet.'

'Wullie, he's brought Dobby up well,' Mum broke in.

'I'll have to take him to complete his training.'

'Yeah, you'll have to contact Fiona and get Dobby booked in for the next block,' she offered, happy to change the subject.

I was also glad Mum changed the subject because I didn't want to get into another dispute about my dog and the hunting instincts of a Jack Russell. He was fine the way he was.

He wasn't brought up on a farm. He wasn't a hunting dog. He was my little house elf. Although I feel I brought him up well, I still had one thing I had to crack.

Chapter 28

SOMETHING CLICKED

Nine months had passed since Dobby had achieved his silver award and it was time to enrol him for his gold. We had been through so much and he was well trained. But he still responded to his granny and grandad more than his dad, so I wanted to be the one to complete his training.

I contacted Fiona to book him in for the next block, starting in late June. She had said that the gold award would take place on a Friday instead of a Wednesday because she had so many classes to run. Dad couldn't take us, so Mum had to step in.

The Kennel Club Good Dog Scheme Gold Award is the highest level of achievement of the scheme. It builds on the skills learnt in the silver award and develops more advanced training skills of the dog and handler.

The gold award is a natural progression of practical dog training skills and introduces new concepts such as *being relaxed* and *settled, stopping the dog, and sending him to bed.* Some new exercises are evaluated at indoor and outdoor locations. I was concerned that Dobby wouldn't answer to any commands because it had been so long since Dobby had been at training.

Fiona had asked Mum to bring Dobby's bed with us when she brought Dobby and me to start the first session of the new block.

'What's this?' Fiona asked, when she had noticed Dobby's harness.

'That's perseverance,' I replied, heading towards a seat set out for us next to the stage.

There were a couple of dogs from before and a few new ones including a collie—a dog that began foundation level at the same time as Dobby. She was once a well-behaved collie, but Covid-19 had affected the dog. She refused to take part in most tasks. She barked if a dog got too close. She barked if her owner strayed too far from her. I felt it was essential to get Dobby used to being on his own for periods because separation anxiety can do that to a dog.

Mum stayed to assist. Tasks included return to handler, stay down in one place, stop the dog and send the dog to bed.

A controlled walk outside was the first exercise of the evening. Mum, Dobby and I set off before everyone else and waited at the gate into Bankie Park. Mum wasn't needed for this one and stood out of the way. Dobby took liberties when he walked with his granny or grandad. His grandad allowed him to sniff on walks. Because he allowed this, his granny often found it difficult at times when she walked him. Dobby walked better with his dad because he knew he wasn't allowed to sniff with his dad.

Mum helped with the exercises we performed inside. *Send the dog to bed* was an easy task. Dobby was in his bed when

Fiona went to pick it up to place it a few yards in front of me. She encouraged him out so she could move it. A bed should be something a dog feels comfortable in but choosing the right one had been problematic. As he had done with the bottom of the backrest of my couch, he had also chewed all of his beds. Once he had stopped chewing holes in leather, I had an idea.

'Do you get synthetic leather beds, Dad?' I wanted to know.

'What d'you mean?' he replied.

'We often thought Dobby would sleep on the couch when he got older and sometimes, he does.'

'Aye, what are you getting at?'

'If he enjoys sleeping on the couch, can we not get a bed which is similar?'

'I'm not sure if you get beds like that, but I'll have a look,' he said.

We had a look when we next visited *Pets at Home*.

'What about this one?' Dad asked, placing a bed in my lap, as he wheeled me around the store.

'Perfect.' I ran my hand over the surface. 'He'll like this one.'

His bed lies in front of the sideboard unit. He often goes in when I ask him to. And sometimes he goes without being told.

'That's a nice bed,' one dog owner from the training class commented.

'That looks like a Pets at Home one,' Fiona said.

'Aye, it's a Three Peaks bed,' I replied.

'Okay, Billy,' Fiona began. 'Send him to bed.'

'Go lie down, Dobby,' I commanded, pointing to his bed.

Slowly, Dobby padded towards his bed, turned around and lay down. A few awws sounded around the hall.

'Excellent,' Fiona said. 'Now call him out.'

'C'mere Dobby,' I said.

He did as I instructed and came to me. If only all of the tasks were as simple.

When it was my turn for re-call, Fiona asked Mum and me to head to the top of the hall. Fiona held Dobby until I was ready.

'Okay, Billy, call him to you.' she instructed.

'C'mere, Dobby.' I pointed beside me.

Saying the command 'c'mere', rather than 'come here' worked when Dobby had off- the-lead walks with his granny and me. Dobby was hesitant but he walked directly to me when Fiona released him. He turned around and sat by my side.

'That was a massive improvement,' Fiona said.

'I've had plenty of time to work on it.'

I didn't think Dobby would manage the next task. This was *Relax settle; move out of sight for two minutes*. In the exam, you didn't have a choice as to which position to leave your dog before you left the room. Fiona chose the position. These were either sit; lie down or stand. He was great at sitting, but not the other two. Mum and I left the room along with the rest of the dog owners while Fiona monitored each dog. She called us back into the room when the two minutes had elapsed. Dobby didn't wander, but he hadn't stayed in the same position.

The last task of the night was *Stop* the dog. This was a task

I found difficult. It was similar to re-call. I spent so long trying to get Dobby to come to me and now I was asked to stop
him. I stood with Mum at the top of the hall and on Fiona's
command, I called him to me. On her second command, I
told him to stop. He didn't.

'You'll have to work on this, Billy,' Fiona said, retrieving
Dobby for another attempt.

'Be a bit more vocal,' Mum said.

'Right, Billy, call him to you,' Fiona repeated.

'C'mere, Dobby.'

He padded towards me.

'Okay, tell him to stop.'

'Stop,' I said, a little louder.

He kept coming.

'Raise your hand,' Mum offered.

'Okay, I'll try it again.'

On his third attempt, he slowed down on my command
but didn't stop.

'You'll get there,' Fiona assured me, calling an end to the
first session.

~~~

In early July, we were now allowed to mix with people inside a pub. I walked Dobby down again, intending to have
a couple of pints and then home. Dobby stopped at certain
points on the pavement and wouldn't move. He wanted to
cross the road where I first taught him to. It hadn't been the
best place to teach him to cross, but he was only doing what
he knew. So, he was really a good boy for stopping. Just at
~~~

the wrong places. He was the same when we stopped at the end of the one-way street. I met a couple of friends in the Royal who were some of my pool players. Dobby lay beside me as we talked.

'How do you fancy coming back to captain the team?' Dan asked.

'I'm out of the loop with pool, now I have Dobby,' I said, picking up my pint.

With the threat of catching and falling ill from Covid at its lowest since the outbreak had begun, the East Neuk Pool League decided to recommence the pool season in September. Dobby was two and well behaved. I could leave him for a few hours now.

'Have a think about it,' Dan continued. 'I can be your second in command?'

'I'll speak to my mum and dad, but they should be okay with it. What about Big Al?' I asked.

Dan backtracked slightly.

'I could be your third in command,' he said.

It was clear that Dan missed the pool season as had I, but I got the feeling he didn't want to commit himself to too many duties. He knew I was the captain who could revive the Royal's team.

'I don't want to demote Big Al if I were to come back.'

'Fair enough.'

'Maybe Big Al wants to stay on as captain?' I added.

'He doesn't,' Dan said.

'How do you know that?'

'He told me. He's done with pool.'

'If I come back, there'll have to be conditions. I'll not be able to stay until the end,' I went on. 'I'll have to go home on the 22:28 bus regardless of if the match is finished or not.'

'Sure,' Dan agreed.

'I won't be able to attend away matches outside Anstruther,' I added.

'Sure,' Dan repeated.

I went outside for a cigarette, and I took Dobby with me. It was difficult getting Dobby through the doors when he was attached to my belt, so I unclipped his lead. He still didn't like my crutches and I had to stand in the correct position, crutches out of the way so that he could go up the two large steps before me. We got there eventually. I allowed him to wander around the beer garden. I found a seat, sparked up and mulled over the prospect of being the pool captain again. There was nothing stopping me going back apart from leaving a dog at home most Wednesday nights. If Mum and Dad were okay with it, then I would go back. But did I really want to leave Dobby at home? After some deliberation I crushed out my cigarette and Dobby followed his dad back inside.

When I sat down, my poo bag holder fell off of my belt. Another man, who stood by the pool table had picked it up. The lid had fallen off and the bag unravelled. He rolled them back together, put them in and screwed the top on.

'Does he get treats?' he asked, handing me the holder.

'Not really, because he has a dodgy stomach. The ones from the bar are okay.'

'What do you feed him?'

'Only kibble and wet food.'

'When do you feed him?'

'Morning and teatime. He gets his tea before, or when I have mine.'

'He shouldn't eat when you eat,' he said.

'Why not?'

'He'll mooch.'

'Not Dobby,' I assured the man. 'He has learned, after he has had his food, he goes and lies down. I have taught him that way.'

'Really?'

'Aye, and if he doesn't, I tell him again and he does. It's a different story with his granny and grandad,' I went on, taking a sip from my pint. 'I've told them countless times to send him away when we eat, but Dad in particular just says, "he's fine." I'm a lot stricter with my dog,' I finished.

The second week of training was similar to the first one. My face muscles tightened when Mum assisted too much. I puffed out my cheeks when she tried to take control too much. I wasn't letting her be like Dad.

I sat sipping from my Holy Grail as I watched the telly the Saturday night after Dobby's second week of training. I couldn't understand it. Dobby was so good at classes. He walked well off his lead with Mum and me. But he would not come in the house when I told him to. The evenings were warm ones. The days were long. He enjoyed taking advantage of the summer nights. But I wanted him inside. I had to be able to call my dog inside when I told him to. The back door was wide open. After a bottle of prosecco, I went to get him inside.

'Dobby, come inside,' I called.

Nothing happened.

'Dobby, come inside, pal,' I tried again.

There was still nothing.

It had to stop. I couldn't continue like this. I left him outside, poured another half bottle into my Holy Grail and messaged Fiona.

'Hi Fiona, I was wondering if we could have a talk?' I typed. 'I'm entering the third week of Dobby's gold training, and I am concerned about something. Would it be possible if you could call me to discuss this?'

'Yes, of course,' she replied. 'Are you free in five minutes?'

'Yes,' I said.

'What's up?' Fiona asked, when I answered her call.

'I still feel that Dobby's answering to everyone but me.'

'Okay,' she said.

'I need that to change.'

'Okay, how can we sort this?'

'Would it be better to train him at classes on my own?' I slurred.

'Absolutely.'

'Would I manage to train him on my own?' I added.

'Yes, of course. I've watched you both. You've done really well with Dobby. There's no reason why you can't complete the training on your own,' she encouraged.

'It's something I feel that I have to do.'

'Where is he just now?'

'He's in the garden somewhere. I can't get the bugger in. I've tried calling him in a few times, but he'll not budge.'

'He's good with you at training,' she continued. 'I've seen big improvements since his foundation level.'

'That's the thing, Fiona. I can't get my head around it. He's brilliant outside with me, but once he's in the garden, he won't come inside.'

'I'll get you and Dobby through his gold.'

'What do I say to Mum?'

'Just be truthful. Tell her that you need to do this on your own. I'm sure she'll understand.'

'Aye, you're right.'

'I'll be there to help if you need it.'

'Thanks Fiona,' I said.

'If I don't hear from you before, I'll see you at class next week.'

It was getting late. There was still a hint of daylight in the sky, despite it being after eleven. I began nodding off. I made one more attempt to get Dobby inside.

'Dobby, come inside,' I said, pointing my finger.

I waited, but nothing happened.

'C'mon Dobby, come inside,' I called again.

He still didn't answer to me. I opened the fridge, removed a bag of cheese and dangled it in the air, but there was still no response.

'Stuff you then,' I roared.

I put lights out. I disappeared into my bedroom thinking he would follow, but he didn't. I lay in my bed for a few minutes expecting to hear little paws. I was sure he would come in.

I woke around six. I reached my hand over to stroke Dobby, but he wasn't there. 'Shit,' I cursed when the realisation dawned on me.

I jumped out of bed and went to see where he was. The back door was still wide open. Dobby stared at me from the arm of the couch. He had come inside while I had been passed out. I gave him a massive telling off. His ears drooped and his tail dropped. I shuffled towards the kitchen and closed the door. Dobby jumped off of the couch, ran through to the bedroom and jumped on the big bed. I didn't like to be angry with him, but he needed to know I was the boss, and he didn't rule over his dad. I slid myself back into bed and we cuddled up together.

I told Mum and Dad what had happened. I didn't find it funny, but they did. I also told Mum that I had spoken to Fiona about completing Dobby's training on my own and she said it would be best if I did.

I checked with Fiona before the next training session to ask if we were starting outside. We weren't, so Mum dropped Dobby and me, along with his bed off at the hall. I thought he would follow his granny to the door, but he didn't.

When instructed, Dobby and I walked around the hall. The other dogs and their owners passed us, but it didn't matter. Dobby walked around the room with me.

'Turn around now guys,' Fiona called.

I stopped Dobby, turned us around and walked in the opposite direction, following the yellow markers against the blue floor.

'Okay, turn around again,' Fiona announced.

We did.

Fiona called a halt to the first task, and we sat down.

The next exercise was *relax settle; lie down;* and *sit* or *stand* for two minutes. Fiona chose lie down. This took some persuading, but Dobby lay down for the full two minutes.

The dreaded re-call was next. He had improved with this one. But how was he going to behave without his granny to assist? Most of the dogs in the class either cantered, ran or trotted to their owner. Dobby opted for a slower approach, but he came straight to me.

'C'mon Dobby, I've not got all day,' I said, and a few laughs followed.

'I think it's because he has adapted to your pace, Billy,' Fiona suggested.

At least he was now following through with his re-call on the first attempt.

Send the dog to bed was the easiest task of the evening. When Fiona asked me to send Dobby to his bed, he did. When I asked Dobby to come out again, he did. A few awws and laughs rang around the room again.

The second to last exercise was to *leave your dog and step out of the room for two minutes.* This was still a task I expected Dobby to fail. Fiona, knowing Dobby sits more than stands or lies down, she told me to ask Dobby to sit. Once he was settled, I left the room. When Fiona asked me to return, Dobby was standing.

'Ah, c'mon Dobby, do as you're told,' I said, crouching, slapping my right thigh. 'You should be able to do it by now.'

Instructing your dog to stop was the final task of the night.

The outcome was still the same, but Dobby was improving. Mum and I had been practising this while on walks with Dobby.

My first session training Dobby by myself went well. I was happier. I was a little more confident that I could complete his training on my own. And Fiona offered me great support.

The following session started outside, so Mum dropped us off at the park and walked us to the far side gate. Dobby suddenly stopped. My brother's van was parked at the kerbside. Dobby recognised it.

'It's okay, Dobby, Uncle Weh isn't here,' Mum said, encouraging him onwards.

Uncle Weh was visiting his girlfriend and Dobby knew he wasn't far away.

'C'mon, Dobby, we'll see Uncle Weh later,' I said, tugging the lead.

Mum left us to it once the class arrived.

The tasks performed outside were the same as inside, but in a larger area. This tempted Dobby to bolt if he had the chance. He came back immediately after talking to other dogs. To stop him from doing this was one of the things you must prevent your dog from doing in order for him to pass his gold training. He didn't run when I trained him in the park.

Control off the lead was one of the exercises we were asked to do outside. Dobby was good at this, but he wasn't quite by my side.

'It's okay, as long as he's in the vicinity,' Fiona assured me. 'That will be enough for him to achieve his gold award.'

Dobby performed well with his training outside and did

the tasks I told him to do, until the end. He decided to go and speak to the other dogs in the class. I thought I had mastered that.

'For fuck's sake, Dobby, did you have to do that?' I roared.

We headed back to the hall to complete the remaining tasks.

~~~

Dobby wasn't eating his food again. I mixed things with his food. I tried torn-up pieces of ham, grated cheese and even broken bone biscuits. I made another appointment with the vet. When we arrived with an underweight dog, the vet came to the waiting room and took him away. Covid protocols still didn't allow you into the consultation room. He wasn't gone for long when the vet returned with him.

'He's just playing you,' she began. 'Dogs can be fussy and look for something better than what you give them. There's nothing wrong with him.'

Both Mum and I turned our heads towards Dobby. My lips flared as his innocent eyes stared back at me.

'What about his food then?' I asked.

'Keep putting it down for him. He'll eat it eventually. Dogs won't starve and they'll eat if they are hungry.'

'Okay,' I said, more satisfied.

I wasn't convinced. But if that's what the vet suggested I do, it wouldn't hurt to try. After a few days, he had no choice—he gave in and ate his food.

~~~

We booked another staycation in early August. This time it was to Newtonmore, a lodge in the highlands. Dobby didn't like car journeys, but he was improving.

It was only a couple of hours' drive to the middle of Scotland. Mum and Dad had booked another dog-friendly lodge called The Den from Monday to Friday. Just like the lodge in Musselburgh, it didn't take me long to familiarise myself with this one.

We took a trip somewhere different each day. The first one was a short drive into Aviemore. Michael and Zuzu had just been to Aviemore the weekend before us. Dobby walked alongside my wheelchair while we browsed the shops.

Aviemore was similar to the Lake District, where I had been on many occasions. It seemed to rain as much in the Highlands as it had done there. We often had to take shelter from the rain as we walked the streets. We happened to stop outside a shop which sold plaques. Mum spotted one with a Jack Russell that said, 'A spoiled Jack Russell lives here.' I bought it and it hangs on my kitchen wall.

We had a longer drive to get to Inverness on the Wednesday. My friend Stuart had told me that there was a good whisky shop in Inverness. Some of my favourites were Glenkinchie, Glengarry and Highland Park but I also enjoyed other whiskies that Stuart had introduced me to. Dad found the shop and wheeled me in. It was indeed a good whisky shop which sold hundreds of bottles, but the prices were through the roof.

Dad picked out a Talisker and carried it to the till for me. It was too expensive and when the woman rang it up,

I asked her to cancel the purchase. The shop was aimed at wealthy American tourists. However, I didn't want to leave Inverness without a bottle, so Dad browsed the shelves again and I opted for a Loch Fyne.

We travelled to Fort Augustus, southwest of Loch Ness, on our final day. There wasn't much for Dobby and me to do on our week away, but the idea with this holiday was to relax for a few days away before putting Dobby through his intense gold exam.

Certain activities were returning to normal. The lower leagues in Scottish football were finally allowing fans into stadiums. These were initially social distanced. This meant Dad and I weren't in our usual seats to begin with.

Dobby had missed one session of his gold training, but a few remained. Fiona started to bring her collie, Star, to classes. Star was an old dog who had been well trained. He sometimes strayed from his spot. Fiona clicked her fingers, and he returned to his position.

Fiona was satisfied with the progress with outside training; the remaining weeks were performed inside. Every task was the same in order to achieve the gold award.

Control walk and *send your dog to bed* were simple tasks and I had no concerns about these. However, Dobby and I had to work extra hard at other tasks in order to pass his gold award. We had to perform *re-call, leave your dog and step out of the room, stay in one place* and *get your dog to stop* to perfection. Fiona tended to keep the difficult exercises for later.

'Okay, Billy, head to the top of the hall,' Fiona instructed.

I walked to the other end, turned around and waited for her command.

'Okay, call him to you,' she said.

'C'mere, Dobby,' I said, clicking my fingers this time. It worked for Fiona, so I tried using the command.

He responded and walked directly to me without other dogs distracting him. If finger clicking helped, perhaps I should try it more often.

'That was excellent.' Fiona said.

Getting your dog to stay in the same position was the next task Fiona asked us to perform. Luckily, she chose *sit*. Asking Dobby to sit was something he always did on my command. Getting him to stay was the issue.

'Dobby, sit,' I said.

'That's him down,' Fiona confirmed. 'Keep him focused on you and move away.'

'Wait,' I said, moving back a few paces.

'Wait,' I repeated, stepping back further.

'Wait,' I said, stepping back for one final time.

I stood with my palm in the air asking him to wait for two minutes and he didn't move.

There were two remaining tasks left, and they were the most difficult ones.

'Okay everyone,' Fiona began. 'Settle your dog in the position I choose.'

Fiona picked a different position for each dog. Knowing Dobby performed better in a sitting position, I had to ask Dobby to sit.

'Okay, leave the room everyone,' she said.

All dog owners congregated in the kitchen until Fiona called us back into the room. Dobby was still where I left him, but he had stood up.

'We've nearly cracked it, pal,' I told him. 'Please stay for Dad,' I added, stroking him.

'I'm sure he'll do the task by the time the assessment comes around,' Fiona encouraged. 'He's almost there.'

The final task of the session was to get your dog to stop. So, when Fiona asked me to go to the end of the hall again, I did. This time I was ready.

'Okay, Billy, call him to you,' she instructed.

'C'mere, Dobby,' I said, clicking my fingers.

He began walking towards me.

'Tell him to stop.'

I raised my palm and as loudly as I could, I said, 'STOP.' And he stopped.

'Call him again.'

'C'mere, Dobby,' I said, clicking my fingers again.

He continued towards me.

'If Dobby performs as well as he has been, he'll achieve his gold certificate,' Fiona offered in my ear once she had brought the session to an end.

A wide grin began to form on my face. We'd almost done it. And on our own. Something I'd strived to achieve since I got Dobby.

There were three training sessions left and I, for the first time, was confident I would complete Dobby's training on my own.

I decided it was time to return to captain the Royal pool

team. I started contacting my players to register a team for the 2021/2022 season. *The East Neuk Pool League* AGM was to be held in the middle of August. Despite encouraging all my players to play for the new captain and not move to other teams, some players had moved on. It had been two years since I'd last captained the team and players were bound to move on. Big Al did recruit new players who I was going to inherit. I managed to get enough players together to register my team. I was still a little cautious of catching Covid, so I didn't attend the AGM.

~~~

The end of August approached, and Dobby's gold award examination grew closer. I had worked hard with his training between sessions. Mum and I also practised commands in the park. I told him to wait while we walked about fifteen yards along the cycle path. He was still in the same place when I turned around. I clicked my fingers and called him to me. Because it worked, I clicked my fingers more frequently. He trotted along and when he was halfway to me, I raised my palm and told him to stop. He did. I clicked my fingers, and he continued towards me.

I had no concerns and was confident when Mum dropped us off for Dobby's exam. All the tasks were performed in the hall apart from the *control walk* on a busy main road. Fiona left that one for last. She asked Mum to come back in time to drive Dobby and me to the top of Banky Park. Fiona would then be able to observe Dobby and me walking along a busy road.
~~~

Dobby performed each task almost to perfection. He was answering to his master—something I never thought he would do. He passed a lot of the tasks with ease. He still struggled with some, but passed them, too. *Stay in one position* was always going to be a difficult one. He passed that challenge. He even performed *stop your dog* and the dreaded *re-call* to perfection. The only exam I was certain he would fail was to *leave your dog in the same position while you left the room for two minutes.*

'He does this one better if you ask him to sit, doesn't he?' Fiona offered.

'Yes, he does,' I said.

Fiona walked around the hall instructing everyone in which position to leave their dog. When she reached us, she asked me to leave Dobby in a sitting position.

'Okay, leave your dog and step out of the room,' Fiona announced.

'Wait there until Dad comes back,' I told him before I followed the rest of the dog owners into the kitchen.

'Okay, you can come back into the room,' Fiona said, the two minutes having elapsed.

Dobby hadn't moved when I approached the spot where I had left him.

'Good boy, Dobby, I knew you could do it.' I roughed him around the ears. 'Well done, pal.'

He looked proudly up at his master, as I held back tears.

'You have all passed,' Fiona said. 'If you can collect your certificate before you leave,' she continued. 'Billy's going to complete his gold with the controlled walk with me. You have all done very well.' Everyone else had already performed the *controlled walk*.

Mum waited by the door to take Dobby and me to complete his final task.

'If you drive them to the tennis courts car park, Joanna, I'll meet you there once I have finished up here,' Fiona said.

We sat in the van until Fiona arrived. She was only ten minutes. Dobby and I got out again and began walking along the busy main road. Usually, Fiona would ask the dog owner to walk a lot further, but the aim was to observe and be confident you were able to walk your dog without any distractions.

Dobby happily walked on my left-hand side along the top of Bankie Park. When Fiona was satisfied, she asked us to turn around and head back. Again, Dobby walked on the inside of me all of the way back to his granny.

'Here comes the golden boy,' Fiona said, approaching Mum.

'Is that him then?'

'Yep, that's him achieved his gold. Billy has worked really hard with him,' she offered.

Dobby stood by my side. My knees buckled listening to Fiona praise how well we had done. I had always been confident that I could train my own dog, but it had to be me who completed his training. A single tear ran down my cheek as Mum and Fiona spoke.

'Aye, they've done well,' Mum said, her voice trembling.

'I'm so proud of them,' Fiona added, trying to hold back her tears.

'Aye, we're all proud of them. They've achieved so much.'

'Okay, here's your gold certificate,' Fiona said handing the sheet of paper to me. 'If there's anything you need, anything at all, just send me a message.'

I was happy to gain Dobby's gold award and receive a certificate, but it wasn't about achieving certificates. The aim was always to be able to train my dog on my own and that was the biggest reward.

The start of the new pool season was also approaching. I had encouraged some players to turn up for practice sessions. I had some new guys and needed to know if they were any good. I was impressed with two young boys in particular. I listened to the balls drop into the pockets while I drank my pint. I learned their voices quickly and put a name to each of them. Josh and Liam were going to fit into my team nicely.

Another two young players were due to start playing for the Royal from the third week of the season. And they were equally impressive.

Mum and Dad had offered to keep Dobby at their house for a couple of hours and put Dobby in my house for me returning after pool. Despite my guarantees that I wouldn't travel to away matches, our first fixture was away from home to the Station Buffet in Elie and I travelled with them.

I was once a great pool player and often beat the best when I had sight and most of my players knew that. I had to give up when playing pool was no longer possible. I decided to be a non-playing captain so that I still had some involvement. The role of captain is to make sure that you have enough players for a Wednesday, pick the team and the order in which you want to play them. But I conducted more than just captain duties. I organised transport for away matches, took care of the admin and treasurer duties among other things. My players were always grateful of what I did for the team and knowing that I used to be a great player, understood my knowledge of the game and appreciated my guidance as captain.

I wanted to make sure my team was ready for the season. It was a difficult start for our first fixture, but it was good to be back captaining a pool team I had missed and loved.

We came away with a narrow defeat, but it would take time to get my mojo back. And I did get my mojo back. We didn't get our first victory until the third game of the season, but with a few of my original plus my impressive new players, we were up and running.

After each Wednesday night, I got the bus home. This was the first time I began using the bus again since the pandemic. I enjoyed my pool night out, but I also looked forward to going home to Dobby. He was so happy to see his dad come home.

Dobby was still a puppy and needed to play. It didn't matter how many pints I had consumed during a pool night, I always made time to play with my dog when I got home. The weather was still warm in early October, so I played with him outside. I threw a tennis ball for him. I rolled around the ground allowing him to crawl over me. If it was too cold, I played with him inside before bed.

Dobby needed to go outside to do his business, but I had once been reluctant to let him out in case I couldn't get him to come back inside. However, once I learned to click my fingers and say, 'In the house,' in he came. I felt confident letting him out at night knowing he would come back in.

I have successfully raised Dobby into a beautiful healthy dog, but none of this would have been possible without the dedicated support and guidance from my family, friends and dog trainer. If I have been able to raise Dobby in the way I have, my perfect companion and I can achieve anything.